"A wily sportsman, a gallant sportsman is the mule deer, every thew and sinew of him, the finest game in all the vast domain he inhabits."
—Donald Culross Peattie, *Sportsman's Country*, 1952

Majestic
MULE DEER

———— ❖ ————

From the Editors of Voyageur Press

Voyageur Press

Majestic
WILDLIFE
LIBRARY

Edited by Todd R. Berger
Designed by Andrea Rud
Printed in Hong Kong

First Hardcover Edition
99 00 01 02 03 5 4 3 2 1
First Paperback Edition
01 02 03 04 05 5 4 3 2 1

Library of Congress Cataloging-in-Publication Data
Majestic mule deer : the ultimate tribute to the most popular game animal of the West / from the editors of Voyageur Press.

      p. cm. — (Majestic wildlife library)
      ISBN 0-89658-413-5
      ISBN 0-89658-538-7 (pbk.)
      1. Mule deer hunting. 2. Hunting stories. 3. Mule deer.
      I. Voyageur Press. II. Series.

      SK301.M32 1999
      799.2'7653—dc21   98-46017
                           CIP

Distributed in Canada by Raincoast Books
9050 Shaughnessy Street, Vancouver, B.C. V6P 6E5

Published by Voyageur Press, Inc.
123 North Second Street
P.O. Box 338, Stillwater, MN 55082 U.S.A.
651-430-2210, fax 651-430-2211
books@voyageurpress.com
www.voyageurpress.com

Educators, fundraisers, premium and gift buyers, publicists, and marketing managers: Looking for creative products and new sales ideas? Voyageur Press books are available at special discounts when purchased in quantities, and special editions can be created to your specifications. For details contact the marketing department at 800-888-9653.

Permissions
Voyageur Press has made every effort to determine original sources and locate copyright holders of the excerpts in this book. Grateful acknowledgment is made to the writers, publishers, and agencies listed below for permission to reprint material copyrighted or controlled by them. Please bring to our attention any errors of fact, omission, or copyright.
"A Time for Muleys" by Charles F. Waterman. Copyright © 1973 by Charles F. Waterman. Reprinted by permission of the author.
"My First Deer, and Welcome to It" from *They Shoot Canoes, Don't They?* by Patrick F. McManus. Copyright © 1977, 1978, 1979, 1980, 1981 by Patrick F. McManus. Reprinted by permission of Henry Holt and Company, Inc.
"I Don't Want to Kill a Deer" by Ted Trueblood. Copyright © 1960 by Ted Trueblood. Reprinted by permission of the Trueblood family and the Ted Trueblood Scholarship Fund.
"White Saddle Buck" from *High Country* by Rutherford G. Montgomery. Copyright © 1938 by The Derrydale Press. Reprinted by permission of Derrydale Press.

Page 1: *A muley peeks from a field of cattails. (Photo © D. Robert Franz)*
Pages 2–3, main photo: *A majestic Colorado buck pauses in a frosty field of rabbitbrush. (Photo © Daniel J. Cox/Natural Exposures)*
Page 3, inset: *A quintet of hunters with their twelve muleys. Fraser River valley, British Columbia, Canada. Circa 1919. (Photo courtesy City of Vancouver Archives)*
Facing page: *Basking in the sunlight late on a summer day, a velvety Rocky Mountain buck beds down until dinnertime. (Photo © Michael Mauro)*
Page 6: *A muley buck with a grand set of antlers. (Photo © James Prout)*

CONTENTS

Introduction

MAJESTIC MULE DEER

Mule deer and their blacktailed cousins are the venerable trophy deer of the North American West. Inhabiting some of the most beautiful country in the world, muleys entice hunters to depart their comfortable homes in the foothills and suburbs and to pursue them at the top of the world, to hunt them in unforgiving desert lands, to battle their way through dense rainforests seeking venison. Majestic mule deer have a power over those inclined to hunt, a power that reaches down from the heavens and grabs ahold of a human being like few other passions can.

Choosing to acknowledge that passion and to pursue muleys or blacktails is a formidable decision. Frankly, it's pretty hard work. But then again, would the mystique of hunting muleys persist if hunters could open fire from their seat at a picnic table? The answer is no. To hunt, as the word implies, means to pursue, often through rugged country, often in unforgiving weather. Often it means going home empty-handed, but satisfied, for the joy of hunting lies in the chase, in the fresh alpine air, in the brief moments when a chance exists that the hunter will kill a mature buck.

With such evocative elements as beautiful landscapes, inherent emotion, and the risk of injury or even death, hunting is a fertile ground for gifted storytellers. Hunting mule deer and blacktails is no exception. In *Majestic Mule Deer* you will read the tales of some of the twentieth-century's best outdoors writers, all of whom were passionate about their pursuit of muleys and blacktails. You will read stories that go a little way toward putting into words why we hunt mule deer, including Charles F. Waterman's "A Time for Muleys," Ted Trueblood's deceptively titled "I Don't Want to Kill a Deer," and Patrick F. McManus's "My First Deer, and Welcome to It," a tall tale of majestic heights that will have you rolling in your Lazy-Boy. You will become engrossed by the tales of deer-hunting days gone by, including Ninetta Eames's century-old story of hunting muleys and blacktails in coastal California, and Rutherford G. Montgomery's "White Saddle Buck," a fictional

Velvety antlers rise above a lush field in the foothills of the Rocky Mountains. (Photo © D. Robert Franz)

story of pursuing deer in the American Southwest in the 1930s. Hamilton M. Laing takes us along on a hunt for blacktails near his home on Vancouver Island, and Elliott S. Barker gets inside the head of a mule deer in a wonderful tale of a hunt from the point of view of the game. Taken as a whole, this unique literary collection provides an engaging portrait of the North American mule deer and the hunters who pursue them.

Majestic Mule Deer is also a folio of images of mule and blacktailed deer from some of the continent's greatest wildlife photographers. The collection features the beautiful work of Mary Liz Austin, Erwin and Peggy Bauer, Denver Bryan, Alan and Sandy Carey, Daniel J. Cox, Terry Donnelly, Gerry Ellis, Michael H. Francis, D. Robert Franz, Lorri L. Franz, Brad Garfield, Curt and Cary Given, Mike Grandmaison, Henry H. Holdsworth, Byron Jorjorian, Layne Kennedy, Michael Mauro, Mark and Jennifer Miller, Bruce Montagne, William H. Mullins, James Prout, Michael S. Quinton, Jeffrey Rich, Sherm Spoelstra, and Michael Wilhelm. In addition to the modern images, historical photographs from throughout the West are interspersed in the text, providing a first-hand look into muley hunting days long ago.

Majestic Mule Deer won't act as a substitute for wonderful days afield; it will simply remind you of the exhilaration of the chase, and make you breathless and impatient for muley hunting season to return. Passion is what the pursuit of game is all about: passion for beautiful country, for venison, for wildlife—for mule deer.

A mature buck with a respectable 4x4 rack. (Photo © Michael H. Francis)

Chapter 1

TO HUNT
FOR MULE DEER

*"To hunt the black-tail with any degree of success, persons must resort
to a dense part of the forest, and if the country is hilly, so much the
better is the opportunity for sport, for the animal seems partial
to a somewhat rugged habitat."*
—John M. Murphy, Sporting Adventures in the Far West, 1879

A TIME FOR MULEYS

by Charles F. Waterman

It is not easy hunting muleys and blacktails. Pursuing game up the side of a mountain or through a rainforest can leave the heartiest of hunters breathless. It is the Herculean effort, as well as a passion for game, that drives hunters to take to the wilderness in pursuit of muleys.

Charles F. Waterman penned books and articles on outdoors subjects throughout a long career as a newspaper reporter, photographer, and editor, and also as a freelance writer. His work has appeared in numerous outdoors magazines, and he was a columnist for the *Florida Times Union* and *Florida Wildlife* as well as for the fishing magazines *Salt Water Sportsman* and *Fishing World*. His books include *The Hunter's World*, *Hunting Upland Birds*, *Hunting in America*, and *The Part I Remember*. "A Time for Muleys" was written especially for the collection *Hunting Moments of Truth*.

There is this special time between brilliant autumn and the forbidding mountain winter. There still are days of rapid thaws, but the Rockies remain white down past timberline and each foreboding snowstorm has a false finality about it as if winter had really closed in.

Most of the potholes are frozen, but mallards slant confidently into steaming spring creeks and loaf on ice edges of the larger rivers. At night there are sounds of Canada geese probing for mountain passes, and most of the snows and blues have already passed on their way south.

Since the earliest deer and elk seasons of September the hunters have sagely stated that the game was high, somehow ignoring the fact that high to low can be a matter of only a few minutes' travel for a deer in case of suddenly bad weather.

The big muley bucks have been hard to find. In late summer some of them could be seen as burly shadows among lesser deer on the alfalfa fields at dusk, and when the season opened a few of them were brought in with pride—but when the first rifle reports bounced through the rocky canyons they had disappeared, as big bucks tend to disappear every fall. They lost interest in alfalfa fields and left most of the valley foraging to does, fawns, and simple-minded forkhorns. The middle-sized bucks were found frequently, but the big ones very seldom.

Pages 14–15, main photo: *Muleys inhabit a stunning variety of habitats, including Colorado's Great Sand Dunes National Monument. (Photo © Sherm Spoelstra)*
Page 15, inset: *A hunting party returns with a blacktail buck. Marin County, California. Circa 1910. (Photo courtesy of The Bancroft Library at the University of California, Berkeley)*
Facing page: *Some muley bucks grow majestic racks, though for the mule deer hunter, a buck such as this often seems more fantasy than reality. (Photo © James Prout)*

Their broad and slightly splayed tracks might be seen in high rimrock, but the beds there would be empty when hard-breathing hunters arrived. Humans give the mule deer little credit for genius, but trophy males are individuals above their fellows in wit. It is not entirely chance that has given them time to grow heavy antler beams and thick shoulders.

There were several seasons when I hunted mule deer a great deal, more than I could afford to, but there was the excuse that we ate hardly any meat but venison for much of the year. My wife, Debie, had a more practical approach than I, and when game biologists reported that more does should be killed she shot one on the first day of one season, only to be treated coolly by hunters afflicted with a big buck complex. She said, with sense, that the food locker was empty and that a young doe is prime meat.

Although the licenses called for two deer I usually approached the magical time between fall and winter without a kill, insisting that I was waiting for trophies, but knowing secretly that I was simply fearful of ending the hunt for another year.

There was the immense satisfaction of lying on a high sage ridge and feeling across the opposite slope with my binoculars to make out bedded deer. When I found one, continued search would almost invariably reveal more sage-hued forms. One slope might take an hour's study, and it was almost a relief to learn there were no worthwhile bucks so that I could go on to another ridge.

One October there was the Montana giant who rested repeatedly in a brushy canyon notch that could be viewed from above, apparently a poor place for bedding, but he could escape like a slipping whitetail through small, thick conifers while I stared watery-eyed at the general area, a chilly canyon wind whipping at my exposed perch. Once I had seen the tines of his antlers moving among some alders along a creek lower down. It took several trips before I learned his favorite escape route and posted Debie there. She caught only one glimpse of a dark, silent form sliding through heavy cover. Several days later she and Jack Ward tried it together, and this time

With the exception of the towering peaks of Alaska, mule deer inhabit nearly all of the great mountain ranges of western North America. (Photo © Mark and Jennifer Miller)

the big buck elected to go with a thumping rush along the canyon wall and Jack's quick .270 caught him center with a single bang while I was still gathering the rocks with which I planned to flush him out.

This other time, Debie, the provider, had collected a butter-fat, rag-horned muley for the locker. We had been looking for elk, and it was late evening with only minutes of shooting time remaining, and she had seen him with several does and fawns feeding in a poorly lighted draw. They sensed her presence and milled uncertainly while she took a steady shooting position, and then they started up a slope, where they alternately merged with juniper clumps and appeared plainly against drab autumn grass. Just below a crest the buck stopped for the muley's risky backward look and she fired once.

The fleeing herd noisily topped the ridge and disappeared, Debie's deer somewhere among them, and I arrived there in a few moments to find her small and forlorn in her bulky wool hunting pants and red shirt. It was almost dark and her deer was gone, she said, but it had looked like a good shot and how could she have missed? With the last light we found the fat buck just over the ridge, but the heavy bullet, chosen for elk, had not opened much on the way through and he had gone a bit farther than was to be expected. Debie was pleased but suddenly announced it was time she killed a trophy.

As the snowy time of the mule deer rut arrived that year I still clung to my two tags and we went to Montana's Madison range. In dead of winter the mule deer often feed fearlessly along the swift, shallow Madison in plain sight of the valley highways. In late November they work up and down the slopes with weather changes. By then most of the hunting camps have been brought out of the highest mountains and outfitters plan to work from headquarter ranches or from permanent camps at easy levels.

It is the up-down movement of deer that can make good hunting for observers of the game. When snow becomes too deep on the upper slopes the deer will move down to feed, but at first they do it mostly at night and return to high and difficult country during the day for alternate bedding and browsing.

There are times when the foothill snow is webbed with trails but no daytime deer are present. As Bud Baker of Ennis explains it, the time for shooting is just after dawn when deer return to higher ground and a hunter who has slipped through them in darkness may cut them off with an ambush. The procedure is simple if the location and weather are right. We have tried it when it had turned too warm and much high snow had melted, and we found only areas packed with tracks where deer herds had been a day or two before. They had temporarily abandoned their valley visits.

In the November I remember so well, four of us left Baker's motel long before daylight. It was Bud and his wife, Mary Ann (for some forgotten reason called "Mike"), Debie, and I. Patches of crisp snow crunched under the four-wheel-drive's lugged tires as we got under way on an empty road, going up the valley in the cold starlight of early morning. One star shone so brightly near the blurred mountain tops that we argued whether it could be a man-made light but decided it was the wrong color for that.

We took a frozen side road and putted past Pete Durham's ranch house, dark and a little apart from the shadows of other buildings, and drew brief but noisy attention from the ranch dogs. We went through the barnyard and through a gate to the steep pasture slope, where the engine labored a little at the beginning of the mountain, and parked there to continue on foot.

On the snowy foothill shoulder were dark blobs of cattle that would wait until we were quite near and then startle us by jumping wildly in apparent terror, only to stop and stare after thirty feet of flight. Once we saw smaller, quicker shadows ahead and knew they were deer, good sign that many of the muleys were "down." After we found the irrigation-ditch crossing we walked carefully to avoid badger holes and were quiet as possible, for we knew we must be passing the deer's feeding areas. Suddenly the peaks ahead of us to the east showed in sharp outline from the very first morning light, and we began to make out the dark streaks of brush and tree-lined draws and creeks coming down the mountainsides from the solid masses of timber higher up. It is those

A young, velvety Montana buck on a brilliant summer day. Antlers encased in velvet are extremely sensitive; muley bucks avoid sparring until the velvet peels in the fall. (Photo © Michael H. Francis)

Above: *The sun begins to set over a muley in the southwestern scrublands. (Photo © Michael Mauro)*

Left: *One ear askew, a buck swivels in the fog toward a foreign sound in the nearby woods. Mule deer have acute hearing, which contributes to the challenge of hunting them. (Photo © Michael Mauro)*

fingers of cover the deer usually follow as they go up and down the mountains, avoiding broad openings.

With growing light we climbed a little faster, our labored breathing marked in puffs of steam, and we crossed a barbed-wire fence where we had made a stand another year. It was by that fence, my back to a rock outcropping, that I had listened to repeated twangings of the wire as unseen deer had crossed it before daylight, but on this later morning we went farther.

We separated to find individual stands. I bore to my left, the others went right. The going got choppier, with rocky patches and juniper clumps easy to see now. Behind me there were yellow specks of light in ranch windows. I reached a point where a shallow draw and its tiny iced creek deepened to a small, bushy canyon with tall timber a little farther up. I sat down on a rock, my outline broken by juniper and stone behind me. Back the way I had come there were scattered patches of timber, and just a little below me on the other side of the creek was a tongue of mature pines, separated from the creek by a wide park. My vision toward the valley was not perfect, but I counted on upward-bound game following the creek and coming within range.

I don't know how long the deer had been standing there. I had glanced about before sitting down and certainly I had been watching for movement, but suddenly he was there, a fat two-point buck, no more than 200 yards away across the draw, standing broadside and watching me. Most deer hunters have experienced the same thing and have wondered if the animal somehow arrived while they were watching somewhere else or if it had stood there for some time and been overlooked.

Deer season was almost over, it would be my last day's hunting, we could use the meat, and the rotund forkhorn certainly would satisfy Debie's kitchen requirements, so I slowly brought the rifle to position, slipped into the sling, and squirmed gently until the crosshairs hung steady behind the buck's shoulder. The shot boomed and rebounded in the canyon, and the deer seemed to have been erased as if he had been an imaginary deer after all. But when the muzzle came down after recoil I made out a gray horizontal form in the weeds where he had stood. The form did not move, so there was no hurry and a big buck might appear later. I faced a little more downhill, checking my first kill occasionally with binoculars, proud of my practical approach.

It was some time later that I first saw the big buck—I had almost concluded that all of the feeding deer had chosen routes that would not pass me. I first saw him as a dot far down toward the Madison as he appeared on a bit of high ground, and I barely focused the glasses before he was out of sight again. Some minutes later he appeared once more, much nearer, and I got a good view of sweeping antlers, thick neck and heavy shoulders. Even then it seemed likely he was heading for my draw, and I studied him whenever he was in view, moving steadily and deliberately up the slope, evidently returning from early feeding but also carrying the belligerent look of a harem seeker on the move. The rut was nearing its end and traveling bucks are common at that time of year, even the giants with little to fear from competitors.

It was some time before I began to estimate ranges. It was 600 yards, I thought, and then he was out of view again and I guessed 500 yards the next time he appeared, but he was coming closer and I started to look for the places where he might make a reasonable target—futile planning, for a deer seldom takes the route you lay out for him unless it is an established trail. He stopped to check the air at intervals as he neared the broken ground below the solid forest. It was broad daylight and he seemed to know he was a little late.

I swung my glasses over surrounding territory, fearful some other member of our party might appear on the slope without seeing the buck, but there was nothing to frighten him. I wondered about scent from me or the others, but he showed no apprehension and the air currents seemed favorable.

Then, after some steady upward progress on my side of the draw, the buck unaccountably turned to move at right angles to it and appeared about to cross. It was a long moment of decision, for there seemed little chance he would come closer. I still estimated he was more than 400 yards away, a hard

Two young blacktail bucks square off near the California coast. (Photo © Jeffrey Rich)

Above: *At least six points per side make this a regal buck indeed. (Photo © Michael Mauro)*
Facing page: *William Clark, of Lewis and Clark fame, wrote in 1806: "The ears and tail of this Animal when compared with those of the [Whitetailed] Deer, so well comported with those of the Mule when compared with the horse, that we have by way of distinction adopted the appellation of Mule Deer." And so it was. (Photo © James Prout)*

choice for one who attempts to hold a personal rule of no shooting past 350. Until then I had remained calm enough, I thought, but the necessity for immediate choice brought my pulse up and the rifle was not quite steady when I sought a rest in a half-prone position against my rock. It was an automatic move, apparently a subconscious decision to shoot, even while I consciously debated with myself. With my hand finally on the rock and the forend on my hand the crosshairs went still and I told myself that only a wild trigger yank could spoil the shot now. I must hold over, I knew, and I put the crosshairs on the walking deer's dark-gray shoulder, then moved them up the distance I felt they should be, only to see he had reached the edge of the little creek and was about

to cross. After the crossing there would be almost level ground, I thought, and he might stop for a look around, so I waited, my thumb checking the safety one more time.

He crossed the creek with a little hop of his front feet and pulled himself up on the level spot, where he came almost to a complete stop, and my finger began to tighten, the bold crosshairs dead steady.

I had not fired when the buck dropped away from my aiming point, falling forward, the great antlers still almost level as the head struck the ground, all in silence, and it seemed a long while before I heard someone else's shot and the bullet's thud. I put down the rifle to look for the gunner and finally saw two red specks far across the wide park and near

the heavy timber from where Debie had shot her trophy buck. The other red speck was Mike Baker, and since my hunting season had ended, I started over to help them dress the kill. It was the best head we have ever taken.

As we came down the mountain with the two deer the sun gleamed on the thread of river in the valley, but it snowed again soon after that and the magical time between fall and winter was gone for another year.

Left: *The snow comes early in the mountains that so many muleys call home. (Photo © James Prout)*
Overleaf: *Mule deer country: Banff National Park, Alberta, Canada. (Photo © Mike Grandmaison)*

MY FIRST DEER, AND WELCOME TO IT

by Patrick F. McManus

Patrick McManus doesn't take writing about mule deer hunting too seriously. In fact, most of his writing exhibits his innate sense of humor. As he told *Contemporary Authors*: "As soon as the humor writer starts thinking of himself as a person of letters, as soon as he perceives his purpose as something other than seeking the ultimate, base, vulgar, gut-busting, psyche-wrenching laugh, he is done for."

McManus' books include *A Fine and Pleasant Misery*, *The Grasshopper Trap*, *Rubber Legs and White Tail-Hairs*, and *The Night the Bear Ate Goombaw*. This piece, from *They Shoot Canoes, Don't They?*, outlines an alternative way to bag a mule deer in a narrative that is pure McManus.

For a first deer, there is no habitat so lush and fine as a hunter's memory. Three decades and more of observation have convinced me that a first deer not only lives on in the memory of a hunter but thrives there, increasing in points and pounds with each passing year until at last it reaches full maturity, which is to say, big enough to shade a team of Belgian draft horses in its shadow at high noon. It is a remarkable phenomenon and worthy of study.

Consider the case of my friend Retch Sweeney and his first deer. I was with him when he shot the deer, and though my first impression was that Retch had killed a large jackrabbit, closer examination revealed it to be a little spike buck. We were both only fourteen at the time and quivering with excitement over Retch's good fortune in getting his first deer. Still, there was no question in either of our minds that what he had bagged was a spike buck, one slightly larger than a bread box.

You can imagine my surprise when, scarcely a month later, I overheard Retch telling some friends that his first deer was a nice four-point buck. I mentioned to Retch afterwards that I was amazed at how fast his deer was growing. He said he was a little surprised himself but was pleased it was doing so well. He admitted that he had known all along that the deer was going to get bigger eventually although he hadn't expected it to happen so quickly. Staring off into the middle distance, a dreamy expression on his face, he told me, "You know, I wouldn't be surprised if someday my first deer becomes a world's record trophy."

A youngster's first buck will reside in the memory right next to a first love. (Photo © Sherm Spoelstra)

"I wouldn't either," I said. "In fact, I'd be willing to bet on it."

Not long ago, Retch and I were chatting with some of the boys down at Kelly's Bar & Grill and the talk turned to first deer. It was disgusting. I can stand maudlin sentimentality as well as the next fellow, but I have my limits. Some of those first deer had a mastery of escape routines that would have put Houdini to shame. Most of them were so smart there was some question in my mind as to whether the hunter had bagged a deer or a Rhodes Scholar. I wanted to ask them if they had tagged their buck or awarded it a Phi Beta Kappa key. And big! There wasn't a deer there who couldn't have cradled a baby grand piano in its rack. Finally it was Retch's turn, and between waves of nausea I wondered whether that little spike buck had developed enough over the years to meet this kind of competition. I needn't have wondered.

Retch's deer no longer walked in typical deer fashion; it "ghosted" about through the trees like an apparition. When it galloped, though, the sound was "like thunder rolling through the hills." And so help me, "fire flickered in its eyes." Its tracks "looked like they'd been excavated with a backhoe, they were that big." Smart? That deer could have taught field tactics at West Point. Retch's little spike buck had come a long way, baby.

At last Retch reached the climax of his story. "I don't expect you boys to believe this," he said, his voice hushed with reverence, "but when I dropped that deer, the mountain trembled!"

The boys all nodded, believing. Why, hadn't the mountain trembled for them too when they shot their first deer? Of course it had. All first deer are like that.

Except mine.

I banged the table for attention. "Now," I said, "I'm going to tell you about a real first deer, not a figment of my senility, not some fossilized hope of my gangling adolescence, but a real first deer."

Now I could tell from looking at their stunned faces that the boys were upset. There is nothing that angers the participants of a bull session more than

On first glance, this buck appears to have a nontypical rack of Boone & Crockett legend. Upon closer scrutiny, his rack separates from the branches of a fallen tree surrounding his hiding place. (Photo © D. Robert Franz)

The unique, bouncing gate of the mule deer is readily apparent with these fleeing does in eastern Oregon's Malheur National Wildlife Refuge. (Photo © Curt and Cary Given)

someone who refuses to engage in the mutual exchange of illusions, someone who tells the simple truth, unstretched, unvarnished, unembellished, and whole.

"Even though it violates the code of the true sportsperson," I began, "I must confess that I still harbor unkind thoughts for my first deer. True to his form and unlike almost all other first deer, he has steadfastly refused to grow in either my memory or imagination; he simply stands there in original size and puny rack, peering over the lip of my consciousness, an insolent smirk decorating his pointy face. Here I offered that thankless creature escape from the anonymity of becoming someone else's second or seventh or seventeenth deer or, at the very least, from an old age presided over by coyotes. And how did he repay me? With humiliation!"

The boys at Kelly's shrank back in horror at this heresy. Retch Sweeney tried to slip away, but I riveted him to his chair with a maniacal laugh. His eyes pleaded with me. *"No, don't tell us!"* they said. *"Don't destroy the myth of the first"* (which is a pretty long speech for a couple of beady, bloodshot eyes).

Unrelenting and with only an occasional pause for a bitter, sardonic cackle to escape my foam-flecked lips, I plunged on with the tale, stripping away layer after layer of myth until at last the truth about one man's first deer had been disrobed and lay before them in all its grim and naked majesty, shivering and covered with goose bumps.

I began by pointing out what I considered to be one of the great bureaucratic absurdities of all time: that a boy at age fourteen was allowed to purchase his first hunting license and deer tag but was prevented from obtaining a driver's license until he was sixteen. This was like telling a kid he could go swimming but to stay away from the water. Did the bureaucrats think that trophy mule deer came down from the hills in the evening to drink out of your garden hose? The predicament left you no recourse but to beg the adult hunters you knew to take you hunting with them on weekends. My problem was that all the adult hunters I knew bagged their deer in the first couple of weeks of the season, and from then on I had to furnish my own transportation. This meant that in order to get up to the top of the moun-

One oversized ear of this Yellowstone doe rotates like a satellite dish. (Photo © William H. Mullins)

tain where the trophy mule deer hung out, I had to start out at four in the morning if I wanted to be there by noon. I remember one time when I was steering around some big boulders in the road about three-quarters of the way up the Dawson Grade and a Jeep with two hunters in it came plowing up behind me. I pulled over so they could pass. The hunters grinned at me as they went by. You'd think they'd never before seen anyone pedaling a bike twenty miles up the side of a mountain to go deer hunting.

I had rigged up my bike especially for deer hunting. There were straps to hold my rifle snugly across the handlebars, and saddlebags draped over the back fender to carry my gear. The back fender had been reinforced to support a sturdy platform, my reason for this being that I didn't believe the original fender was stout enough to support a buck when I got one. My one oversight was failing to put a guard over the top of the bike chain, in which I had to worry constantly about getting my tongue caught. Deer hunting on a bike was no picnic.

A mile farther on and a couple of hours later I came to where the fellows in the Jeep were busy set-

ting up camp with some other hunters. Apparently, someone told a fantastic joke just as I went pumping by because they all collapsed in a fit of laughter and were doubled over and rolling on the ground and pounding trees with their fists. They seemed like a bunch of lunatics to me, and I hoped they didn't plan on hunting in the same area I was headed for. I couldn't wait to see their faces when I came coasting easily back down the mountain with a trophy buck draped over the back of my bike.

One of the main problems with biking your way out to hunt deer was that, if you left at four in the morning, by the time you got to the hunting place there were only a couple of hours of daylight left in which to do your hunting. Then you had to spend some time resting, at least until the pounding of your heart eased up enough not to frighten the deer.

As luck would have it, just as I was unstrapping my rifle from the handlebars, a buck mule deer came dancing out of the brush not twenty yards away from me. Now right then I should have known he was up to no good. He had doubtless been lying on a ledge and watching me for hours as I pumped my way up the mountain. He had probably even snickered to himself as he plotted ways to embarrass me.

All the time I was easing the rifle loose from the handlebars, digging a shell out of my pocket, and thumbing it into the rifle, the deer danced and clowned and cut up all around me, smirking the whole while. The instant I jacked the shell into the chamber, however, he stepped behind a tree. I darted to one side, rifle at the ready. He moved to the other side of the tree and stuck his head out just enough so I could see him feigning a yawn. As I moved up close to the tree, he did a rapid tiptoe to another tree. I heard him snort with laughter. For a whole hour he toyed with me in this manner, enjoying himself immensely. Then I fooled him, or at least so I thought at the time. I turned and started walking in a dejected manner back toward my bike, still watching his hiding place out of the corner of my eye. He stuck his head out to see what I was up to. I stepped behind a small bush and knelt as if to tie my shoe. Then, swiftly I turned, drew a bead on his head, and fired. Down he went.

I was still congratulating myself on a fine shot when I rushed up to his crumpled form. Strangely, I could not detect a bullet hole in his head, but one of his antlers was chipped and I figured the slug had struck there with sufficient force to do him in. "No matter," I said to myself, "I have at last got my first deer," and I pictured in my mind the joyous welcome I would receive when I came home hauling in a hundred or so pounds of venison. Then I discovered my knife had fallen out of its sheath during my frantic pursuit of the deer. Instant anguish! The question that nagged my waking moments for years afterwards was: Did the deer know that I had dropped my knife? Had I only interpreted it correctly, the answer to that question was written all over the buck's face—he was still wearing that stupid smirk.

"Well," I told myself, "what I'll do is just load him on my bike, haul him down to the lunatic hunters' camp, and borrow a knife from them to dress him out with." I thought this plan particularly good in that it would offer me the opportunity to give those smart alecks a few tips on deer hunting.

Loading the buck on the bike was much more of a problem than I had expected. When I draped him crosswise over the platform on the rear fender, his head and front quarters dragged on one side and his rear quarters on the other. Several times as I lifted and pulled and hauled, I thought I heard a giggle, but when I looked around nobody was there. It was during one of these pauses that a brilliant idea occurred to me. With herculean effort, I managed to arrange the deer so that he was sitting astraddle of the platform, his four legs splayed out forward and his head drooping down. I lashed his front feet to the handlebars, one on each side. Then I slid up onto the seat ahead of him, draped his head over my right shoulder, and pushed off.

I must admit that riding a bike with a deer on behind was a good deal more difficult than I had anticipated. Even though I pressed down on the brake for all I was worth, our wobbling descent was much faster than I would have liked. The road was narrow, twisting, and filled with ruts and large rocks, with breathtaking drop-offs on the outer edge. When we came hurtling around a sharp, high bend above the hunters' camp, I glanced down. Even from that distance I could see their eyes pop and their jaws sag as they caught sight of us.

What worried me most was the hill that led down to the camp. As we arrived at the crest of it, my heart, liver, and kidneys all jumped in unison. The hill was much steeper than I had remembered. It was at that point that the buck gave a loud, startled snort.

My first deer had either just regained consciousness or been shocked out of his pretense of death at the sight of the plummeting grade before us. We both tried to leap free of the bike, but he was tied on and I was locked in the embrace of his front legs.

When we shot past the hunters' camp, I was too occupied at the moment to get a good look at their faces. I heard afterwards that a game warden found them several hours later, frozen in various postures and still staring at the road in front of their camp. The report was probably exaggerated, however, game wardens being little better than hunters at sticking to the simple truth.

I probably would have been able to get the bike stopped sooner and with fewer injuries to myself if I had had enough sense to tie down the deer's hind legs. As it was, he started flailing wildly about with them and somehow managed to get his hooves on the pedals. By the time we reached the bottom of the mountain he not only had the hang of pedaling but was showing considerable talent for it. He also

Above: *The plains and badlands of western North Dakota harbor spectacular mule deer bucks. (Photo © Michael H. Francis)*
Left: *An Alberta forkhorn pursues an itch. (Photo © Jeffrey Rich)*

seemed to be enjoying himself immensely. We zoomed up and down over the rolling foothills and into the bottomlands, with the deer pedaling wildly and me shouting and cursing and trying to wrest control of the bike from him. At last he piled us up in the middle of a farmer's pumpkin patch. He tore himself loose from the bike and bounded into the woods, all the while making obscene gestures at me with his tail. I threw the rifle to my shoulder and got off one quick shot. It might have hit him too, if the bike hadn't been still strapped to the rifle.

"Now that," I said to the boys at Kelly's, "is how to tell about a first deer—a straightforward factual report unadorned by a lot of lies and sentimentality."

Unrepentant, they muttered angrily. To soothe their injured feelings, I told them about my second deer. It was so big it could cradle a baby grand piano in its rack and shade a team of Belgian draft horses in its shadow at high noon. Honest! I wouldn't lie about a thing like that.

The majesty of a mule deer buck in the Colorado Rockies. (Photo © Erwin and Peggy Bauer)

In most states and provinces, hunting season ends before the mule deer rut. (Photo © D. Robert Franz)

In much of their Canadian range, including the territory of this buck in the Rocky Mountains of Alberta, mule deer must co-exist with wolves, a successful predator of muleys. (Photo © Michael H. Francis)

Chapter 2

MULE DEER COUNTRY

"Glorious! Two miles beyond that point the grassy plain broke up into a wild revel of bad-lands, such as delights the heart of a mule deer, and a deer hunter. The whole landscape was hacked, and gouged, and cut down into a bewildering maze of deep canyons and saw-tooth ridges, all thinly sprinkled over with stunted pines, and junipers and cedars. As far as I could see, to right, to left and straight away, the wild and eerie bad-lands bespoke mule deer, and beckoned us to come on."
— William T. Hornaday, "Diversions in Picturesque Game-Lands," 1908

DEER HUNTING ON SANHEDRIN

by Ninetta Eames

Mule deer, including their blacktail cousins, inhabit some of the most spectacular land in the world. From the Great Plains on up the majestic Rockies to the Pacific coast, from the deserts of Mexico to the rainforests of coastal Alaska, mule deer habitat is a varied terrain perhaps unmatched anywhere on earth. They share their mountains, rainforests, and deserts with wildlife ranging from gray wolves to armadillos, animals which contribute immeasurably to the atmosphere of hunting these elusive deer.

Ninetta Eames took to the coastal mountains in northern California to pursue muleys. A turn-of-the-century western writer whose work appeared in *Harper's New Monthly*, *Overland Monthly*, *Out West*, and other periodicals of the day, she was also friends with another northern California writer, Jack London, and went on to write several articles about the famous author.

"Deer Hunting on Sanhedrin," which was first published in 1897, is a wonderful account of deer hunting days gone by in a spectacular landscape.

Sanhedrin or Sanhedrim, as the mountain is locally called, is a noble eye-rest for the California traveler, from whichever way he approaches its wilderness of peaks and pines. History does not tell us who gave to this interesting landmark its musical Jewish name, but it was my good fortune to run across an old hunter who told how, in the early fifties, one Pierre de Léon, an educated Frenchman, came to live with the Indians hereabout, and how when troubles arose between the several tribes, a council of chiefs took place on this central mountain, and De Léon, who was present, was said to have begun an eloquent speech with the declaration, "We are the Great Sanhedrin of the Nomalackie tribes."

The name thus dramatically introduced into Indian nomenclature, has since clung to the traditions of this vast "council-chamber"—Nature's "Hall of Gazzith"—whose superb appointments of tree colonnade, rock sculpture, cloud-picturing fountains, a rich mosaic of flora for pavement, and the whole burnished heavens for roof, fit it more for the meeting

Pages 42–43, main photo: *Mule deer inhabit a truly astonishing variety of landscapes, from the rainforests of the Pacific coast to the deserts of the southwest, from the mountains of the Canadian north to the American Great Plains. This doe winds her way through the South Dakota Badlands. (Photo © Layne Kennedy)*
Page 43, inset: *Mule deer country above Banff, Alberta, Canada, in 1924. (Photo by Byron Harmon. Courtesy Glenbow Archives, Calgary, Alberta.*
Facing page: *The sun sets behind an eastern Wyoming buck. (Photo © Sherm Spoelstra)*

place of gods than for white hunters or Diggers in war-paint.

Viewed from the Russian River valley, Sanhedrin runs its ten miles of noduled ridge against the northern blue, its height hardly less than the snow-scarred cones of Mount Hull, St. John, and Snow Mountain. This group of Coast Range summits forms the upper apex of a rugged spur whose trend is from northeast to southwest, the whole including what is known to the few as the best deer preserve in California.

When, therefore, Sam Paxton and Doctor George wrote to us to join them in their regular summer's hunt on Sanhedrin, the invitation was gladly accepted.

There were five of us in the party, with hunting equipments, saddles, blankets, and "grub-box," all snugly packed in a stout spring wagon and cart. Pedro, the Doctor's deer-dog, shared the backseat with the Commodore. Not one of us, unless it be Pedro, is likely to forget that morning's drive out the orchard lane and on up the long, shining valley with its dimplement of river blue, the wind sweet and cool in our faces, a broad sunrise brilliance on the mountains, and all the shaggy wild-wood of the foot-hills gathering to us. Sixteen miles on up stream, and we trace the Russian River to its head in Potter Valley, where modest farm-homes peep at the passers-by through loops of hop-vines and windows framed in apple-boughs.

Beyond the peaceful valley the road turns leftward to let us squeeze between the steepled bowlders that overlook Coal Creek. Thence on we zigzag across broken uplands, down whose gardened cañons the snow treasures of Sanhedrin come cascading to the south fork of the Eel River.

At this season the Eel River has a summer flow measuring no greater depth than reached our wagon-bed. But winter shows a different phase—a foaming torrent impossible to ford; and the occasional pilgrim to Sanhedrin solitudes must submit to be swung across from bank to bank, in a basket hanging from a cable.

Six velvety bucks bedded down in a grassy field. (Photo © Michael Mauro)

Above: *Some particularly "majestic" ears are highlighted in sharp relief when backlit in a Wyoming scrubland. Muley ears can stretch outward as much as ten inches (25 cm). (Photo © Michael H. Francis)*
Facing page: *The forests of immense trees in California's Sequoia National Park are home to many muleys, including this young buck. (Photo © Byron Jorjorian)*

In climbing out of Day's Vale, our interest in the landscape grew apace; we were beginning the ascent of Sanhedrin. The forest became denser—not massed in solid shades, but grouped in beautiful open groves, the dark plumes of conifers in lovely contrast to the foliage of oak and madroño and the pale green of hazel.

High and still higher we mount, every foot of the ascent bringing fresh wonderment at the vastness and grandeur of the mountain world about us. The colossal gap between us and Mount Hull and Iron Mountain is the roadway of Eel River, its lofty walls smoothed out of jagged feature by sweeps of forest and chemisal, the whole as wild as if newly created. At times we catch the glint of water from depths of gorge. We lunch by a bowlder-choked stream, and eat the thimble-berries on its banks for dessert. After an hour's rest we are again on the road.

This glorious wilderness is a choice feeding-ground for deer. The broad forests on the east and south of Sanhedrin are, as yet, practically inaccessible to lumber traffic, and no pick of miner has defaced the comfortably-cushioned rocks. Even stock-raising is at a disadvantage, as the snow lies so late on these alpine highlands that only migratory flocks and herds come up from the valleys to graze in the short warm season.

The deer's favorite browse is chemisal—"chemise brush" it is commonly called; the name is supposed to be of Indian origin. Whole mountain fronts grow this thorny, dull-colored shrub, and, shortly after the uninviting pasture has been swept by fire, deer greedily feed upon the sprouting twigs. These high woodlands also furnish unlimited supplies of other browse—leaves, buds, shoots, moss-fiber, acorns—any of which deer prefer to the sweetest of young grass. When winter sets in, small bands, led by masterful old bucks, work their way gradually down to warmer

altitudes, keeping as much as possible to sheltered passes.

Each steep we gained—hunters assert there are twelve distinct summit-ridges to Sanhedrin—was housed and dreaming under living towers of cedar and pine. I have never seen mightier specimens of these trees in the Sierra or northern Coast Range than are marshaled here in stalwart clans four thousand feet above sea-level.

We wound up the south slope of the mountain, through mile above mile of primeval forest. The sun darted javelins through the dim vault of the trees, the young oaks clapped their leaves joyously, there was a spiced coolness in the air, and the vigorous splash of Cedar Creek made tumult in the ravine that walled in the road. A sign-board was nailed to an obtrusive fir, and the Commodore hailed us to "heave to till he made out the colors."

Our "sailor man" spelt out the straggling letters of "Bachelor's Camp," and the horses were turned off the road, when they crashed uphill through a tangle of berried shrubbery. A few rods of this, and the great pines stood aside to make room on a sunny glade for sapling oaks. Sam and Burk were already here and unloading the cart. There were two hours yet of sun, and we all turned to at the jolly work of regulating camp.

Nature seemed to have done the planning for us, and with a felicitous regard for the relations of beauty and utility. You saw at once which niche she intended for the dining-room, the sun-proof boughs of a fir for ceiling, and walls of interlocked alder and pepperwood. A kitchen square alongside had an indoor water supply to delight the heart of the most exacting housekeeper. While Sam energetically proportioned off the stream into "spring-house," sink and cellar, the Doctor was intent upon building the kitchen-range, his hands fitting the rocks and clay-mortar with the nicety of a stone-mason. In the meantime the Commodore constructed table, benches and stools, the boards having been brought from a little mill a mile up the divide. Burk and I busied ourselves at various odd jobs, and finally settled to cutting fir-boughs for beds.

When it came to getting supper, Sam naturally fell into place as head cook, his experience in the army and in many a summer's hunt since, making him exceptionally expert in outdoor cooking. Add to this a painstaking knowledge of woodcraft and deer-lore, with unfailing good humor and helpfulness, and Sam's virtues as a comrade may be readily understood.

While we lingered over supper, a young man with two hunting-dogs rode up and handed us a can of fresh milk. There were general "how d'y' dos" and hand-shakings, followed by the eager question:

"Seen any deer lately, Jimmie?"

The answer was not so encouraging as we expected:

"There was plenty awhile back, but last week a couple o' 'Frisco hunters was all up an' down here an' Panther Cañon, a-shootin' every digger-squirrel an' chipmunk they see, so of course scared off a lot o' deer."

Jimmie could not wait just then to further advise us; he said he "guessed he'd better git a move on, as them girls was alone at the cabin"—meaning his wife and sister—but he promised to guide us to the best hunting on the mountain.

After the exertion of the day, we were tired and sleepy, and made little ceremony of hurrying to bed. Our tent was spread in the upper chamber of the grove, and in all the magnificent castle of out-of-doors there was never a more inviting or convenient apartment. Two giants, a pine and a fir, upheld the stately arch of doorway through which we looked down upon the "lower story," our eyes fascinated by the weird night-effect of the scene. The smoldering fire lit fitfully the cavernous dark of the kitchen, where Sam's gaunt form moved to and fro, setting things to rights. Outside the dim circle made by the light, the black trunks of the trees stood like a stockade, and beyond them the immeasurable gloom of the forest.

One novelty in our tent was a miniature well, a foot or two wide and of equal depth—a break in the crust of earth above an underground stream. We had our bed directly over this stream, and from my

"Few wild creatures are as versatile and successful as North America's deer. Whether shaped by the ineluctable processes of evolution, the cleverness of Grandfather Raven, or the wisdom of God, deer are a paragon of genius in wild design."—Richard Nelson, Heart and Blood: Living with Deer in America, *1997. (Photo © Alan and Sandy Carey)*

pillow I could dip my cup into the fern-fringed bowl.
I lay back in an ecstasy of privacy and rest, my limbs
acquainting themselves by slow degrees with the
yielding, fragrant mattress, and my senses deliciously
lulled to sleep by the tinkle of the running brook.

The next day we spent in overhauling traps and
straightening up camp, lazying off a bit now and then
in the irresponsible way that is half the charm of
out-door living. Near sunset Sam shouldered his
rifle, and with Pedro at his heels, sallied forth to satisfy himself of the whereabouts of deer, for we
planned an early hunt in the morning.

In Northern California, and more particularly
Mendocino, the chase is usually carried on with
trained hounds, some of which cost their masters no
inconsiderable sum. A sheepman willingly gives one
hundred dollars for a good "varmint dog," and often numbers six to a dozen in his pack.

A shepherd-dog is generally considered the best
for deer, though a cross with a foxhound and a bloodhound will often produce a mongrel superior to either parent for deer-hunting. "A dog can have too
good a nose," as Sam expressed it; that is, a pure
bloodhound will cause delay and trouble by sticking too long to a trail.

There are two varieties of black-tail deer—
Cariacus columbianus—found to-day on Sanhedrin:
the forked-horn Pacific or Coast deer, and the
"sprangled"-horn, the latter by far the more numerous.

When Sam sauntered into camp an hour or two
later, our neighbor was making his nightly call with
the milk. Sam asked him "Which way had we better
go in the morning?"

There was a momentary scratching of the dark,
curly pate.

"Well, I reckon we jump more deer down on the
river, an' that's your best chance. Last time me an'
my wife was there, she says, 'There lays a deer!' An'
sure 'nough there was a big 'sprangled'-horn buck,
an' 'long side o' him a yearling. I had only Dad's old
Winchester, but I let fly an' jest shaved the old feller's
rump, an' he lit downhill fifty feet at a jump, an' I

*Washington's famed Mount Shuksan towers over mule deer
country in the Mount Baker–Snoqualmie National
Forest.(Photo © Terry Donnelly)*

lost him. Cap and Spot [his two dogs] headed off the little spike till I got in a shot an' killed him. It had something cur'ous 'bout it; its horns was hard with the velvet on. I never see one that-a-way before."

It was agreed that the four of us should call for Jimmie as soon after daybreak as possible, Burk promising to stay and keep camp. Accordingly, at four in the morning, I was jarred awake by something like a bomb exploding close to my ear. It was Sam, whooping outside the tent. The Commodore snorted, sleepily, "Ay, ay, sir!" and then floundered back to bed, and drew the blankets over his bald head. This would never do. I lit a candle, and stuck it with melted tallow to a box, then felt for his neck-band, and shook him till his eyes stood out, and he bawled lustily, "Belay that!" After this effectual "eye-opener" we both hurried into our clothes and joined the others in the firelight.

A hasty breakfast was eaten, while Pedro stood about, his eyes and tail eloquently mindful of what was in prospect. When we took the guns from their cases and made a start for the horses, the intelligent brute trotted from one to the other of us in an exuberance of understanding; he was as sure of the hunt as if he already scented the game.

The morning broke with perfect weather, the wide blue of the sky propped by ponderous peaks, the risen sun a glory on the world, a breeze waking to music the vibrant pines, and every falling stream a tuneful undertone to infinite harmonies. It was not so early but a digger-squirrel scurried over the dry leaves and cones in ostentatious search for his breakfast of pine-nuts. The bark of this plebeian of the *Sciuridae* is so evidently an impertinence, that one is provoked to silence it even at the risk of putting to flight nobler game.

We rode single file down the mountain. When we reached Jimmie's cabin, the family was eating out-of-doors, the dogs nosing about the legs of the table.

The delay at the cabin was a short one, as Jimmie's horse was saddled, and soon he was in advance, piloting us over a south exposure of wild mountainside to the Eel River canon. We spoke under our breath, as deer are keen to detect the human voice, but are often indifferent to sounds made by cattle and horses. In this rough-country hunting a horse is used as much as possible to lessen the labor of the chase. Sam's Billy seemed to enter quite as intelligently into the sport as his master, who related instances where he loaded one or two deer on him and then sent him alone back to his partner in camp, while he—Sam—continued the running down of a wounded buck.

When well over an intervening ridge bristling with chemisal, Jimmie called the dogs after him and struck out alone down the river to make the drive with the wind. A deer's sense of smell is so acute that the greatest caution is necessary to keep to leeward, until he is brought by the hounds within range.

For some silent minutes the rest of us walked our horses on an obscure trail midway up the slope, where we overlook a sweep of upper and lower hillsides and ravines. On crossing a verdant dip where springs gush, we see sharp-toed hoof-prints, and judge that five deer at least have been here to drink within an hour. Thence on, our excitement and eagerness augment with every step, and our eyes rest searchingly upon each object that bears a likeness to the game.

Suddenly the hounds give tongue—a portentous outburst which the mountains catch and give back in a thousand stirring echoes. With bounding pulses we urge our horses toward a group of oaks. Sam hears Pedro's prolonged, mournful bay in the lead, and cries exultingly:

"He's jumped a deer! Just hear the music. Now for luck, boys."

They are grand—those urgent, death-thirsting yells, which make cataracts of our blood! Flinging ourselves out of stirrups into the shade, we tie up quickly; then with rifles held so as to clear the chemise brush, we stumble heedfully over the lip of the scarp. Sam is on ahead, and as Pedro's trumpet challenge grows nearer and more furious, keeps calling to us in an extravagance of relish, "Listen to that music! *Isn't* it beautiful?"

We are all equally enthusiastic, but the Commodore seems at a loss to understand. He glows with sympathy, but is evidently confused. His eyes

With a neck thick from the rut and a coat as luxurious as a heavy, woolen blanket, a beautiful buck searches for does on a cold November day. (Photo © Alan and Sandy Carey)

wander from point to point in a puzzled way, and when Sam again exclaims, "Just hear that chorus, boys! Great guns, but that's the music for me!" he bursts forth:

"Music? I don't hear any music! If those dogs would keep still, I might."

It was said in all simplicity, but Sam looked such daggers of disgust that I hastened to interpose by asking where each of us was to be stationed.

Sam's ardor had received a heavy shock, and his answer is cold and straight to business:

"You and the Commodore stay where you are. Doc, you had better get up on that big rock below, and I'll go still farther down to those trees."

Sam is a general at a deer-drive, and we obeyed without question. From our several vantage grounds within hallowing distance of each other, we commanded the mouths of three small ravines which opened into the main defile of the river. A deer is not apt to run across a cañon, but up or down it; and, judging from the direction the dogs were heading, it was certain the Commodore and I would get the first shot.

A few minutes' breathless waiting, and then a mad plunge through brush, and the bump-bump of bounding hoofs, a startling glimpse of flying horns and dun hide, and the clamorous hounds break cover within a hundred yards of us. Bang! my bullet over-flies the mark by a good foot—a common mistake in downhill shooting, and the Commodore, who had never before seen a wild deer, stares open-mouthed and forgets he has a gun. Crack again! A curl of blue smoke below us, and the Doctor gets off his pedestal with more haste than dignity, and running across a strip of open ground, disappears behind a parapet of rocks.

We made the precipitous descent at breakneck speed, coming upon the scene just as the Doctor was imperturbably shifting the position of a big buck so as to turn the head downhill, that the blood might better run from the gaping wound in the throat. The dogs, panting but elated, crowded around us, and Sam coming leisurely up, the bullet-hole was pointed out to him.

"Phew! Spine cut in two as clean as a whistle. Doc ain't much of a hunter, but fetch along our deer and he's the best running-shot in the country."

The Doctor's jolly laugh set the woods agog, and a blue jay, perched on the polished red of a madroño bough, squalled vociferously in company. We all voted the buck a noble prize; fat, glossy of rump, and with an imposing frontlet of soft horn wrapped in beautiful mouse-gray velvet.

The next thing in order was the pouching of the deer for packing. The skin was split down the back of the front legs from knee to dew-claw, the knees then unjointed, and the limp ends crossed diagonally and used as toggles through the slit gambrels of the hind legs. By this ingenious manipulation the hunter adjusts the carcass to his shoulders as he would a knapsack, and is thus enabled to carry the weight with the least possible friction and fatigue.

After an exhausting scale of the hot cañon wall, each of us taking turns at packing the deer, we emerged from the jungle of chemisal to the sheltering oaks, where Jimmie was waiting with the horses. The sun being now high, we were of one mind to return to camp to refresh and cool off. All were as hungry as cannibals, so it was a great relief to find that Burk had the dinner well under way when we got there, and Sam had only to put the finishing touches by doing to a turn some venison steaks. His practiced fingers delicately disposed the floured pieces in the smoking grease, and the appetizing odors that arose made my mouth water. Burk puttered about the wood-pile, and the Doctor in brown "Mother Hubbard" overalls, a flowered calico neckerchief knotted loosely around his neck, a towel slung over one arm, and a long steel fork held ready for use—cut a comical figure as second cook.

"Deer liver" declared Sam, "ain't really meat, but hunter's bread. I've cut it just like a loaf and spread butter on. If cooked right, you can't eat enough of it to hurt you."

That night, for a late supper, we had deer meat in another form—a "digger roast," as the boys called it. A saddle of venison, sprinkled with salt, was rolled in greased brown paper, and dipped in water. The logs of the fire were then pushed back, a hole dug in the hot ashes, the roast fitted in and covered with live coals. During the hour it was to remain we sprawled before the blazing pitch-pine, a forest of

A Colorado buck seems to bask in the sunshine. (Photo © Michael Mauro)

Above: *Five regal bucks make their way through an agricultural area in California's Lower Klamath unit of the Klamath Basin Wildlife Refuges along the Oregon border. (Photo © Jeffrey Rich)*
Facing page: *Along with the forests and mountains, mule deer are at home under the Big Sky of the American plains. (Photo © Michael Mauro)*

firewood to our hand, and the whole night—the all-contenting, star-hung night—before us.

When the dusk was deepening, Jimmie's wife came along with our nightly supply of milk. She laughed at our fears to let her return alone through the woods, and after a grateful "good night," both horse and rider were swallowed up in the black of the forest. The Doctor looked after her, with uneasiness:

"It doesn't seem just right to let her go alone!"

As if in answer to the kindly thought a ringing note of song reached our ears, the words indistinguishable, the air wild and musical. It was repeated again and again, each time sounding fainter and sweeter through the hushed pines.

"She is nearly home," said the Doctor, as he gave a relieved poke to the fire.

Shortly after we had a picturesque intruder—an old hunter, called "Dad." He was well known to the boys, who made him heartily welcome. Dad had on the conventional overalls, a gray flannel shirt, minus a button at the neck, and a faded vest, with a whole row of buttons off. His old felt hat might have been the original, so battered and full of holes was it. He seated himself upon one end of the long bench, and the Commodore sat cross-legged on the other, both doing their best to balance their seat on the hummocky floor. Then we drew our visitor on to a graphic recital of how he killed the biggest panther ever seen on Sanhedrin—a ferocious beast that measured over nine feet from tip to tip and weighed two hundred pounds.

In his excitement Dad rose to better slap his thighs, the bench gave a vicious tilt, and behold, the Commodore's legs beating a wild tattoo in the air as he keeled completely over!

For four consecutive mornings we rode to various hunting-grounds, all within five miles of camp

and only once came back without bigger game than quail and grouse—the latter a splendid game-bird, slaty-blue in color and as large as a domestic hen. We kept to "station-hunting," there being less work about it, and more certainty of success. The biggest kill we had was the morning the Doctor shot three deer, all before they could run a hundred feet. That day the camp was overstocked with venison—four deer strung up to the same stout limb. We made a handsome divide of spoils with Jimmie and the men at the mill, and as a team happened to be going through to Ukiah, sent a choice hind quarter to a friend there.

I had my first luck over beyond Windy Flat, with the Doctor and Pedro to make the drive. On making the ascent of a pine-tipped steep, we came upon a couple of deer-beds—two oval depressions, each about three feet long. The soil and leaves inside were worked up fine and pressed down by plump bodies, and the signs of recent occupancy so fresh that we half believed the beds were yet warm. Pedro scented the trail, and his tail went up.

We agreed to work down the south fork of a cañon, which spread its arms at our feet. The long hollows and hillsides were skirted with copses that deer love to haunt, and bowlders, moss-spotted and whiskered, were tumbled on the sunny patches between. Sam stationed himself on a furzy shelf across the stream, and stood erect, gun in hand, as fine a figure of a mountain hunter as one cares to see. The Commodore stood his ground directly opposite, where he fidgeted and perspired like a man hard beset. As a sportsman he was from first to last a self-confident failure, but not once did he lose pluck and energy.

From my position midway I faced a romantic glen whose summer foliage was all alight and murmurous. Anon was the rap-tap-tap of that little carpenter, the woodpecker, or the cheerful clatter of quail in the hazel brush, but altogether it was tedious waiting. At last Pedro opened—a faint bellow, but fast growing louder and fiercer. I knew the honest fellow was talking deer, for he never gave a false alarm, and so my fingers played nervously with the trigger.

A typical buck in Colorado's Rocky Mountains. (Photo © Mark and Jennifer Miller)

Columbian blacktails call the Queets River valley rainforest in Washington's Olympic National Park home. (Photo © Mary Liz Austin)

Then came the sharp report of Sam's rifle. I thought, "There goes my chance," when crash! thump! an antlered head broke from behind a rock not a hundred yards off, and with no consciousness of taking aim I blazed away. I saw that I had winded him, for he stumbled and turned from sight downhill, by which I judged him hard hit; for a deer severely wounded is sure to drag himself gulchward.

I ran to see, and Pedro, leaping the runnel below, I signed him to the spot. He bounded ahead, and, when I came up, was having a spirited bout with a six-pointer, the buck half lying, but making desperate resistance with his sharp horns and hoofs. The knife ended it, Pedro muttering savagely meanwhile.

Sam, too, was not to be outdone that morning. He had brought down a two-pointer; so we considered ourselves well repaid for a long forenoon out.

To Sam is due the credit of shooting the one Pacific forked-horn seen by us on the trip. The fifth morning he went off on a still-hunt to Summit Lake—a pond or deer-lick seven miles from our camp, on Cedar Creek. He returned by middle of the afternoon, and the buck he had slung across Billie was altogether the largest we had yet come upon, and its horns the handsomest. We drew closer to demand particulars.

"I guess it was just a 'happenstance,'" Sam said, with an adroit wink and thrust of his tongue. "Generally a man don't wait to see a deer, but just shoots at what might be a part of one—a patch of brown or gray, the bush above a pair of slim sticks that look like legs, or somewhere below two tips of ears or a bit of horn that the sun strikes. One time a bowlder I'd been watching, up and jumped twenty feet in the air, an' plunged downhill like an avalanche; so there's something in knowing a deer when you see it. But this time I had a whole broadside to aim at, an I tell you it was a picture—smooth an' fat, head up and

Antlers seemingly as wide as the horizon adorn this Colorado muley. The Rocky Mountain mule deer generally has larger antlers than its whitetail cousins. (Photo © D. Robert Franz)

horns branching, ears flaring an' the shiniest eyes staring straight ahead. I wished I could see him in the short blue—then a buck's the prettiest animal in the world. I knew he couldn't scent me, so I lay low a spell to watch him. Well, it wa'n't long before he concluded he hadn't heard anything, so he up with his hind hoof an' scratched his ear, an' then fell to browsing. Have you ever noticed how a deer can't keep still a second? He kept shaking, stamping an' wiggling his tail, always fighting the fleas and buck-flies. I didn't dare wait too long, so I drew a bead an' took him back of the shoulder."

We helped string up the buck, and then all hands napped in the shade for a couple of hours. When I roused up, there was Sam methodically at work on his deer—cutting off the head, separating the horns from the skull, and skinning the carcass—lamenting, meanwhile, that he had not done the last while the animal was yet warm.

"Comes a sight easier," he said, and then showed me what I persistently try to forget is there—the nest of maggots always secreted in the cavity just below the eyes in a deer.

"Ugh! that's worse than a ship's biscuit," the Commodore exclaimed.

Despite eternal vigilance on the part of a deer, a fly gets up its nostrils and lays eggs, with the result related.

When Sam had made a neat job of the dressing, he proceeded to sack the deer—"put on its nightgown," as the Doctor had it. He first whittled out a peg, and punched a hole in the bottom of a burlap sack. Then drawing the string that held the deer up through the hole, he passed the end around the limb of a oak, pulled on the cord, and swung the venison out of reach of the "varmints."

"You see," he explained with complacency, "by punching the hole instead of cutting it, the mesh

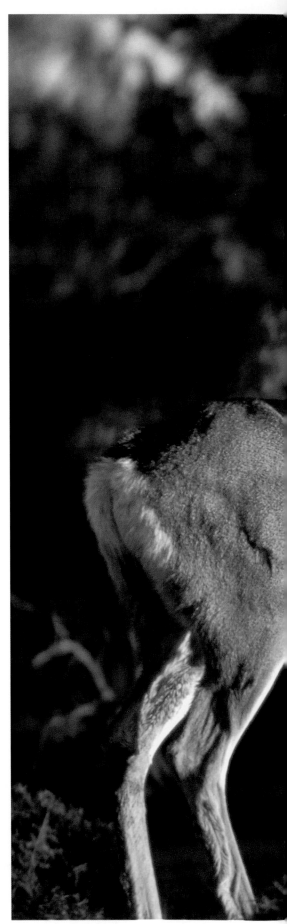

Above: *Hopefully this Rocky Mountain fawn will grow into its ears; though given the youngster is a mule deer, its Opie Taylor look is not likely to diminish. (Photo © Denver Bryan)*

Right: *Scientists contend that the mule deer is really a hybridized species resulting from the mating of blacktails and whitetails some 7,000 to 14,000 years ago. (Photo © Gerry Ellis/ENP Images)*

Southeast Alaska is home to the diminutive Sitka blacktailed deer, one of two species of blacktails. (Photo © Jeffrey Rich)

closes tight around the string and keeps out the flies."

Sam was a master at handy tricks. But the sack did not reach more than half-way down, so he drew another sack over the exposed parts that it overlapped the first, and then secured it by baling rope about the middle.

The day came all too soon for the Commodore and me to leave Bachelor's Camp, the rest of the party having decided to stay yet a week longer. By getting an early start, we would reach the nearest stage-line in time to catch the down coach for Ukiah, and thence finish our journey by rail—one hundred and fifty miles from Sanhedrin to San Francisco in one day.

On our last night a crescent moon rocked in the gap between two fir-pinnacled domes. A subdued radiance stole abroad, and the profound stillness of the mountains was better than music to soothe one. We wandered happily under the sugar-pines, above

whose swinging tops the stars flashed through thin, voyaging clouds. Such armfuls of scented cones as we carried to camp for that last night's burning! They were the largest I ever saw, measuring all the way from fifteen to eighteen inches in length, and when piled artistically, made the prettiest, crackliest camp-fire imaginable.

We were up at three in the morning, and by four o'clock had breakfasted and harnessed the horses. The Doctor was elected to drive us down Sanhedrin—a risky undertaking, for as yet no streak of dawn pierced the thick forest on Cedar Creek. Sam and Burk did their best to give us a cheerful send-off. They built a pyramid of gummy cones at the head of the road, and put a match to it when we were ready to start. The Doctor mounted to the front seat, took up the reins and whip, and set one foot on the brake; and while Pedro howled and tugged at his chain, I climbed up beside his master.

At the final moment Sam seized the handles of

Alert muleys keep a wary ear out for trouble. (Photo © Curt and Cary Given)

two blazing cones, the Commodore snatched a couple more, and in the general illumination the procession began a reckless dash, down grade, Sam's spectral figure running on foot in the lead, his torch held high, the Commodore prancing after and brandishing his flaming cones till the fiery smoke and sparks trailed back like the tail of a comet. It was wildly fantastic and exhilarating—the illusory figures of the two men, the weird lighting of the road, which looked like a tunnel through the pits of blackness upon either hand, the dumb challenge of highwaymen boles as they stepped forth and retreated with startling abruptness—our wheels grazing the unflinching granite on one side and the brow of a frightful abyss on the other, and overhead the pale stars slipping from sight one by one.

At times a dead pine, preternaturally tall and white, menaced us with fixed, ghostly arms, or a prostrate, disjointed fir reared its hydra-headed roots, like a dragon threatening us as we tipped crazily toward its ambush. When Sam's torch gave a dying flicker, he tossed it over the cliff and threw up his arm with a shout of farewell. The horses plunged ahead, and I looked dizzily back; nothing could be seen of our friend, only a second's glimmer of the yet burning torch—a star flung into infinitude.

We stopped for the Commodore to get in. He had carried our beacon bravely until both hands were blackened and scorched with burnt pitch. The Doctor cracked his whip at the off horse. It did not seem possible for mortal eyes to be sharp enough to keep the restive brutes in that ribbon of road. I made myself as small as I could, for our driver appeared to need all the seat. His heavy body, with the elbows held well out, balanced from right to left, the shoulders bent a trifle forward, his hat pushed back and eyes bulging with their intent lookout. With gasp and unfinished sentence, I clung to the farther end of the seat, the Doctor gently but firmly insisting that he must have "elbow-room."

It was like trying to keep to one place in a cyclone. We lurched from right to left, spinning around sharp angles, plumping into gutters, lunging ahead up rocky steeps, always a desperate dodging of shadowy trees which set themselves determinedly in our way, and then a final lightning race down a precipice with a dismembering "fetch-up" at the bottom. We timed ourselves from "Oat Gap" to the foot of the mountain—a long four miles—and found we had made it in fifteen minutes. It was the most superb feat in mountain-driving I ever witnessed.

Foraging can be trying when the snows come. (Photo © Michael Mauro)

I DON'T WANT TO KILL A DEER

by Ted Trueblood

Ted Trueblood wrote for the American sportsman, penning numerous articles for *Field & Stream*, *True*, and *Elks Magazine*. He authored many books on outdoors subjects, including *Ted Trueblood on Hunting*, *The Ted Trueblood Hunting Treasury*, *The Hunter's Handbook*, and several on fishing.

"I Don't Want To Kill a Deer" first appeared in *Field & Stream* in 1960. The piece not only wonderfully portrays the experience of hunting in mule deer country, giving the sights, sounds, and smells of the land a certain texture, but also explores the inner motivation that drives one man to hunt.

I don't want to kill a deer. I haven't really wanted to kill a deer for years. Yet I go deer hunting every fall and have, I suppose, shot about as many of them as most other men my age. If these statements constitute a paradox, bear with me.

Consider October, the hunter's moon. The heat of summer is over. The September rains have washed the haze of August from the air, and frosty nights have brought the first dusting of gold to the white-barked aspens. In all the arid West, from the Coast Range to the eastern slope of the Rockies, the shimmering, lovely days of Indian summer have laid their spell upon the land.

The early harvest is finished, but the orchards are still flecked with the rich red of late apples. The voice of the cornfield has changed from the whisper of summer to the dry rustle of autumn. The stubble, from which the grain had long since been taken, has the look of fall about it, and the young cock pheasants that it harbors are rapidly acquiring the full glory of their adult plumage.

Everywhere, especially in the cool of evening, the rich, ripe, fruity odors of the season lie heavily upon the air. Late-curing hay; grapes hanging purple from the vine; the rich earth, disturbed to yield its treasures; melons, frost-sweetened and dead ripe—all these and many others add their savor. And always, somewhere in the distance, an eager householder, unable to wait for the deluge of leaves that will come later, is burning the first sprinkling. The smoke, thin and clean, drifts low across the countryside. It adds spice to all the other mingled odors, seasoning them with the sure proof that this is indeed October.

At this time we go hunting. It is a tradition. Our preparations are made pleasant by memories of past trips and anticipation of the one ahead. We are going to hunt deer, not merely kill them. The reward is in the hunt, but since there could be no hunting were there no deer, and

A mule deer buck and doe in California's Tule Lake National Wildlife Refuge. (Photo © Jeffrey Rich)

since the logical culmination of any hunt must lie in securing its object, we will no doubt kill one.

Thus rifles and food and bedrolls and tent are loaded, and we drive away from the rich, green valley into the brown foothills and through them, winding always upward, into the home of the mule deer in October. Yellow pines stand majestically alone on the south slopes, their trunks brick-red in the late sun. Aspens line the draws along the clear brooks that trickle down, and make bright splashes of yellow among the dark firs on the north hillsides.

Camp is made, water carried from the little stream nearby, a fire kindled. Soon the heartening odors of good outdoor food and coffee mingle with the tang of the smoke that rises in a thin, straight column toward the earliest stars. We eat and loaf beside the embers and plan the morrow. This first evening, loaded with anticipation, is a real part of deer hunting, and we enjoy it to the fullest.

We will hunt a country we know well. It is always a challenge to explore a new area, but it is also rewarding to hunt where you know each ridge and valley, where every little bench and pocket holds its share of memories. Here beside this patch of timber I missed a big buck in 1936. With a forkhorn, two does, and two or three fawns he had walked out of the thick cover just at sunset. He was very close, and I thought, "I'll shoot him in the neck," but somehow I missed. I saw the bullet kick up the dirt behind him, a little to one side, and before I could work the bolt he leaped back among the trees and disappeared.

And down the draw from this saddle is where another fine buck eluded us by running low along the bottom, screened by alders and aspens, until he was out of range.

On this bench, several deer have fallen to our rifles during the years. And down the canyon below it, where alternate thickets vie with more open browse among the boulders on the hillsides, many fine bucks have rewarded us.

There are real, as well as sentimental, values in hunting a familiar country. You know where to look for deer that are trailing through on their annual migration from the high summer range to their lower wintering area. You know the pockets where they hide during the day. You know where to look for the resident deer that spent the summer here rather than higher in the mountains. And you have learned through experience the best way to approach all these places without alarming any game that might be in them.

The alarm rang at 4 o'clock. I crawled reluctantly out of the warm sleeping bag, touched a match to the fat pine slivers in the little sheet-iron stove, lit the gasoline lantern, and dressed. Then I stepped outside. The snapping stars were so close that I could almost touch them; not even the palest hint of gray showed in the east. There were slivers of ice in the water bucket. I slopped a little into the wash pan, and by the time I had applied it to face and hands no trace of sleepiness remained.

It is during these magic hours that a hunter has the best chance to see deer undisturbed in the open. In the early morning, usually not later than 8 o'clock, they gradually feed or wander into some tight and hard-to-approach thicket where they will spend the day. About sunset they emerge to feed again.

The grass was crisp underfoot as I walked along the bench east of camp. The mountain on my left loomed black against the northern sky, and since I couldn't possibly see a deer anyway, I hurried; I had about a mile to walk and I was chilly. I wore no coat because I knew it would be warm later, but now the air was sharp.

The eastern sky grew paler, and finally there was a hint of pink and saffron to give sure promise of approaching day. Individual trees became visible on the mountainside. I knew I'd soon be able to see a deer. I slowed down and attempted to walk quietly. The spot where I wanted to be at shooting time was just ahead.

Here a little stream came gurgling down out of the hills. Its drainage was a basin, perhaps a mile long and half that wide, divided into several draws and pockets, with steep ridges between. There were bare slopes and brushy ones, dense thickets and sparsely covered benches. It had everything—food, water, thick cover, and shade. During migration the deer—which followed a course generally parallel to the river in the bottom of the valley and did most of their traveling at night along the open slopes facing it—turned into this basin to spend the day. Here, finding things to their liking, they sometimes loitered for a week or more if the weather remained pleasant.

I paused at the mouth of the basin to test the wind.

Above: *Mule deer country: Pyramid Lake in Jasper National Park, Alberta, Canada. (Photo © Bruce Montagne)*
Left: *An eastern Wyoming buck. (Photo © Sherm Spoelstra)*

It was perfect, a steady, downstream breeze. I crossed the brook and started slowly up the game trail a few yards above it on the other side. It was now light enough to shoot. I took a few careful steps, paused to examine everything in sight, took a few more steps, and paused again. I tried not to make a sound.

Time was when I hunted mule deer from the ridges. I could watch a big area and cover more ground, and there was less chance of alarming the game. Lately I've come to favor walking up a valley. I can't see so much country, but what I can see, I see better. I have to hunt more carefully, but any deer I see is usually in range.

I moved slowly along, alternately watching and walking. The predawn chill, which my brisk walk across the flat had overcome, caught up with me again. Shivering, I hung my rifle over my shoulder and put my hands into my pockets to warm my fingers. The light grew stronger, and at last the sun touched the highest tip of the high ridge on the west.

I was looking at it, anticipating its warmth— though the best of the hunting would be over by the time the sunlight reached the bottom of the valley— when I saw a movement halfway up the slope. It was in sparse brush along the point of a ridge that came straight down toward me from the peak. On the right, on the north slope of this ridge, was a dense stand of firs. On the left, extending toward the mouth of the little valley for several hundred yards, was a sparse stand of mixed snow brush, ninebark, and chokecherry, with clumps of bunch grass in the open spots.

The movement could have been made by a bird or a squirrel—or by the flick of an ear. I watched carefully but saw nothing more for several seconds. Then suddenly a deer stepped from behind a cherry bush. It was a long way up the slope. I raised my rifle slowly and looked at the animal through the scope. A doe. Does were not protected, but I had no desire to kill one, at least not this early in the hunt. Our best venison has always come from big bucks killed before the beginning of the rut.

The foothills of the Rockies, from northern Canada to Mexico, are home to the mule deer. (Photo © D. Robert Franz)

A Columbian blacktail forages in the shadow of Washington's Olympic Mountains. Blacktails have a much longer history than their mule deer cousins, having evolved from whitetails as long as two million years ago. (Photo © Jeffrey Rich)

An early season snowstorm doesn't seem to phase these veteran Colorado bucks. Some mule deer in the far northern reaches of their range have actually had their exposed ears frozen solid when the temperature plunges. (Photo © Mark and Jennifer Miller)

I lowered my rifle and continued watching. Soon a second deer materialized, farther out in the brush. It was no bigger than the first, and I assumed that it was another doe or a small buck. Then, almost at the edge of the timber, a third deer stepped leisurely from behind a clump of ninebark, moving slowly toward the trees. Even before I could raise my rifle to look at him I knew he was the one I wanted. I could tell by his size and by the way he walked that he was a big buck. I got the scope up barely in time to get a glimpse of him before he disappeared. His rack was big; certainly each antler bore the four points of a mature mule-deer buck, and maybe more.

The chill was forgotten. I sat down in the game trail and watched the edge of the timber until the sunlight reached the bottom of the valley, hoping he would come out. He didn't. The two other deer, one a small buck, went in.

Thanks to having hunted here before, I didn't have to walk on up the valley and inspect that patch of timber to learn how big it was. I knew all about it. It covered ten acres or so, from the top of the high ridge on the west to the creek in the bottom, and it ran from the crest of the hogback down into a ravine on the north. It was big enough to hide a hundred deer, and it would be impossible for a lone hunter to push any of them out—or get a shot if he did.

There were several things I might do. I could go on hunting and forget about the buck. I could continue up the creek and climb the hillside to inspect a bench north of the timber in the hope that the deer might have gone on through. I could, of course, work my way into the jungle and hope for the best.

None of these possibilities seemed very attractive. I felt sure that the little band of deer had gone into the timber to spend the day. When evening came they would emerge, and with luck I might be in the right spot waiting.

Back in camp by 9 o'clock, I cut some wood, started a stew that would be ready when my partner came, and looked around for any other odd jobs that needed doing. Twenty yards from the tent, the bench on which we were camped broke away sharply to the river bottom. I walked over and looked down at the

Two bucks in a Montana wheat field. (Photo © Denver Bryan)

This mule deer buck is alert during the rut on a western North Dakota ridge. Muleys don't range much further east than this. (Photo © Michael H. Francis)

river, sparkling among the cottonwoods. Its voice, muted by distance, rose and fell softly with the vagaries of the breeze.

The jobs didn't seem very important and the blanket of pine needles on the ground was soft. I decided to sit down in the mellow sunlight and look at things. I thought about the spots where the big buck was most likely to come out of the timber and wondered whether I should go fishing—the trout season was still open. And then I decided to sort of lie back on the needles for a minute or two and put my cap over my eyes.

My partner woke me as he came in. He had seen only tracks. We ate and discussed the possibility of getting a shot at the big buck in the evening. Two of us

would have a better chance than one, since there were several spots where the three deer might emerge, either to feed or to continue their leisurely migration toward the winter range.

Northwest of the patch of timber was a low saddle over which deer often crossed into the drainage of the next creek. A hunter stationed there would also be able to watch the bench that bordered the timber on the north—a likely spot for them to feed in case they decided to loiter a few days in the little valley. If they intended to continue toward the winter range, however, they would be more likely to come out of the south side of the timber, probably near the spot where I had seen them in the morning, and swing around the points of the ridges that dropped sharply down toward the river.

The high point above the timber, where I had been looking at the sunlight when I first saw them, was the apex of several ridges. The good browse bordering the timber extended around to the river slope in the pockets between the heads of the ridges. It would be worthwhile to watch those pockets.

We left camp in late afternoon, not retracing my path of the morning but walking up the next creek to the west. This way we could reach our chosen stations without forewarning the deer, because the breeze regularly drifted up each valley in the evening. When we were a little beyond the saddle, we climbed the hillside nearly to it. Here we separated. My companion would find a position from which he could watch the hillside, the bench on the other side, and the northern and western edges of the timber.

Gradually climbing higher, I angled back toward the southern point of the ridge, staying on the west side opposite the timber. Eventually I reached a spot from which I could watch a couple of brushy pockets, above and just around the corner from the southern edge of the cover. I couldn't see the cover—I was afraid to go around because the upcanyon breeze might drift my scent into it—but any deer that came out should eventually wander into my view.

I had barely settled myself down to begin my vigil when I heard a shot. Just one. It was back where I had come from. It could be nobody but my companion, since there were no other hunters in the area, and one shot usually means a dead deer.

Instantly I was torn by indecision. Had he killed the big buck? Should I go back to help dress it or should I stay here? Was there any chance of the buck's coming out now, assuming he was still alive? Well, if I returned I certainly would not get a shot, whereas if I stayed I might. So I leaned back against the hillside with my rifle across my lap and devoted my attention to the pockets below me. They were partly floored with grass and partly grown up to several varieties of browse. I searched them minutely and, satisfied they were vacant, allowed my attention to drift off across the valley.

This was the magic hour, when the night creatures begin to stir and game feeds in the long twilight. Instead of the keen anticipation that I should have felt, however, the ordeal of holding still bore heavily upon me. I was assailed by doubt. I sat there quietly while the sunset blushed and faded.

Imperceptibly the shadows grew thicker; it would soon be too dark to shoot. For the thousandth time I began a careful examination of the two pockets below me. And there, suddenly in full view and close, stood the buck of the morning! How he arrived unseen was a mystery, but of his presence there could be no doubt. Nor did I have any question as to his identity. He was magnificent.

He was standing broadside, but his head was turned slightly away and he appeared to be looking at something farther down the little basin, perhaps at another deer that I couldn't see in the deep shadows. Slowly, quietly I raised my rifle and eased off the safety, holding it with thumb and finger so that there would be no click.

Twenty-four hours earlier I had harbored no particular desire to kill a deer. I would hunt, yes, but I was not anxious to kill a deer. Twelve hours earlier I had seen this buck. and immediately, as though ordered by some remote ancestor whose very life depended upon the hunt, I had devoted every faculty to bringing about this very moment. Now, partly because my planning had been sound, but to a much greater degree because the buck had been unlucky enough to come into the open at this particular place and time, I was about to kill him. Without thought, without an instant's hesitation, I centered the crosshairs on his gray neck and squeezed the trigger.

Above: *Time to snooze for this rut-exhausted buck. (Photo © Erwin and Peggy Bauer)*
Facing page: *This velvety buck sports a remarkable set of nontypical antlers. (Photo © Brad Garfield)*

Chapter 3

THE CHASE

"What possessed me I knew not. . . . My eyes searched avidly the bush-dotted ground for my quarry. The rifle felt hot in my tight grip. All inside me was a tumult—eager, keen, wild excitement. The great pines, the green aisles leading away into the woods, the shadows under the thickets, the pine-pitch tang of the air, the loneliness of that lonely forest—all these seemed familiar, sweet, beautiful, things mine alone, things seen and smelled and felt before, things. . . . Then suddenly I ran right upon my [mule] deer, lying motionless, dead I thought. He appeared fairly large, with three-point antlers. I heard Copple's horse thudding the soft earth behind me, and I yelled: 'I got him, Ben.' That was a moment of exultation."
—Zane Grey, Zane Grey's Book of Camps and Trails, 1922

TIPTOEING IN BIG TIMBER

by Hamilton M. Laing

Exhilarating is the adjective that best describes the chase for muleys and blacktails. It is the very essence of the hunt: the pursuit of game. There is no guarantee of success, of course, but the heart-pounding elements that make the chase so thrilling are what calls most hunters to the wilderness. To actually get a deer is simply icing on the cake.

Hamilton "Mack" Laing knew well the thrill of the pursuit of his favorite game—blacktailed deer. Born in Ontario, Laing led a fascinating life that was as varied as it was successful. He worked as a rural teacher in Manitoba, studied art in Brooklyn, served in the Royal Flying Corps during World War I, worked as a naturalist for the Smithsonian Institution and the National Museum of Canada, and operated a nut farm at Comox, British Columbia, where he settled in the 1920s. A prolific writer as well, Laing published some nine hundred articles on hunting, nature, and travel. "Tiptoeing in Big Timber" first appeared in the March 1936 issue of *Field & Stream*.

I admit it—I am a head hunter. Much as I like the satisfaction of a juicy, well-hung venison steak between my molars, I enjoy more the sight of a good antlered trophy fairly won. In my deer hunting I have killed but one young spiker, and that was under stress of compulsion.

My victims must have passed their majority and show worthy head-gear. The bigger they are the better, even though I must truly "grunt and sweat under a weary life" in packing them out. Like the Ancient Mariner, I do my penance for my folly; but instead of albatross about my neck, a blacktail is draped for hours upon my sagging shoulders. In the years to come, when wabbling knees must fail to take the logs under such load, I know there will be satisfaction to sit and look above the fireplace, and, in contemplation of well-mounted trophies, live again the heart-thumpings of the hunt.

I make no excuses, yet because of some knocks handed the head hunter I feel that a word can be said for his failings. The antlered monarch, be he moose or deer or caribou, is liable to be beyond the pale as good food. You might as well take old Toros from the dairy herd at the height of the season of his usefulness and expect him to furnish good meat. As a matter of fact, in taking the veterans from the woods where already they have made their mark, giving

Pages 84–85, main photo: The pursuit of mule deer will often lead you to snowy heights. (Photo © Michael Quinton)

Page 85, inset: A hunter approaches his kill near Cabri, Saskatchewan, Canada, in 1970. (Photo courtesy Saskatchewan Archives Board)

Facing page: A doe peeks through a new forest in early autumn. (Photo © Denver Bryan)

place to younger males, you may be doing nature a favor.

It was mainly because of my friend Smith that I invaded a new hunting ground in quest of that biggest blacktail head and went tiptoeing in the green woods up Dove Creek. "Cougar" Smith had been up there early in October and had come back with a tall story.

"The biggest buck I ever saw on Vancouver Island!" was the verdict.

On an open bluffy slope toward the creek he had seen this veteran; but having two hounds on leash, he was a bit handicapped. The net result was a shower of hair mixed with the scenery and the intended victim did his next quarter of a mile in very long jumps. There was not a drop of blood.

Now Smith has seen not hundreds, but even thousands of deer in these woods. After making due allowance for the twinkle in his eye, I judged that he had seen a big buck with a head which would make that fall memorable. It was a year when heads were exceptionally good; all the hunters agreed on this.

"He was that wide across the prongs! Oh, he was a moose of a deer!" declared Smith.

Though Vancouver Island blacktails have poor horn spread, still I believed him.

It was a sunny late-October day. A forest primeval with fresh hoof-prints on the old deer trails—what more could a hunting heart ask for? I had once been through this stretch of woods, which as yet lay far ahead of the logger, and knew a little of the lay of the land—its green bluffs, its sunny salal slopes with mossy-rock outcroppings, its high peak with the tiny lakelets, the open face breaking down toward the singing creek—the most perfect spot for blacktails that could be found in these vast green woods.

I figured that by now the big bucks that had summered high in the interior would have worked down into this area. It seemed certain that at least one was here somewhere. Though Smith intimated that probably the big fellow had not quit running yet, I was not discouraged.

Someone else had had an eye on this hunting ground, and had blazed a trail—no, just a way—leaving it blind where it came out to the pack trail leading up from the auto road. In his endless wanderings in quest of panthers, Smith had found out about this and posted me. A fine thing, I thought, till I tried to follow it. Being blind at the other end also, it was distinctly a one-way trail. I never came out on it.

The low morning sun was just touching the green-mossed rocky abutments on the point of the first ridge when I paused to search the woods on three sides. Here was an extensive view of a hundred yards—rare in these dense woods. Blacktails are on the move till 9 A.M. Toward November, as they begin to feel desire for companionship, the bucks prowl much later.

And there he was! Down on the very point of the ridge a gray something moved. It caught the sunlight a fleeting moment and once again, then passed behind the big firs. A buck for sure, when he marches steadily along like that—had I been two minutes later, we must have met. Though I tiptoed down there quickly, I saw nothing more of him.

Nor was I more successful through the hours. In all the silences of these great woods—in the shadows or on the more open sunny slopes of green salal where timber was smaller—I found no sign of my buck. But I saw seven deer, does and their young; and it tickled my vanity that only two of these saw me first. The other five I could have shot—and did: with the safety on. It is good practice, keeping eye, hand and nerve in training for the big moment.

"I thought so," said Smith when I told him. "It's always that way. In a week or ten days the bucks will be there."

So November was a week gone when next I scrambled up the blazed way to the ridge. With the thought of that big one carrying the cougar hunter's trademark on him somewhere, I began the usual breathless stealing in these green forest aisles—that most fascinating game of stalking in the timber, where a hunter is ever on his toes and every sense in him is a-tingle.

I had figured on sunlight, but the day disappointed me. Given the sun, I can outguess a buck eight times out of ten. He will be in a comfortable spot warming his back as he takes his mid-day rest. Having lost that trump, I circled off over a new course which, I judged, would about noon bring me to the steep back of the highest ridge.

Deer sign, yes, there was no doubt of those trails and the droppings among the salal, but these bucks were sly ones. My stomach was crying "Noon!" As I

A troika of bucks is interrupted mid-forage on a sunny June day. (Photo © Alan and Sandy Carey)

stopped and examined some panther kills of last winter, I saw, across a narrow swamp, the back of my ridge, but not a hair had I seen or heard thump of bounding blacktail hoofs. Then I heard it— *clack-crock!*

The startling sound was close; surely that was the whacking of antlers. Two bucks must be sparring just at the foot of the ridge. *Crack-clack-plok!*

I strained eyes and ears. Once before in these woods I had been badly fooled. Then I decided it was only the chopping of the log-cock, and my heart settled down again and blood-pressure came back to normal. Yet I could see no woodpecker or any stub in that direction. Still I listened, till the suspense got

the better of me. As I moved across the swamp there was a sudden rustling tumult in a thicket of small hemlocks and something big went out of there in a hurry.

One of the rarest sights of the woods under my nose, and I had muffed it! My day was spoiled. When the list of various kinds of fools that I called myself was exhausted, I panted up the steep hill and hunted the other side. There was half sunlight there, but the little open park held no sign of deer. Then, just as I left it, I saw quite close below me the gray side of a black-tail. A buck—I felt sure of it.

His head was down, poking in the salal. Then be

Above: *Columbian blacktails, such as this California spikehorn, have a coastal range from northern California to southern British Columbia. (Photo © Jeffrey Rich)*
Left: *Sitka blacktails, which inhabit a limited range in southeast Alaska, closely resemble whitetailed deer in many respects. (Photo © Erwin and Peggy Bauer)*

raised it. Yes, there were horns on his crown—the thin yellow points of a two-year-old. He was sleek; as he moved, his fat sides seemed to ripple. Fifty yards. I slowly raised the rifle, covering his neck, then put it down again.

Something held back my reluctant hand. I wanted him, and I didn't. Then he settled the matter by letting out a sudden disdainful snort, and in one hop he was over the bluff. Human-like, I wanted him more now, but though I hurried to the brow I saw nothing of him again. He blew his nose mockingly away below.

Ordinarily it is my rule to hunt away from the trail till midday and hunt homeward through the short afternoon, but now I worked on into new territory. Soon I made out another deer below me. In a little park-like bench a hundred yards off stood a very big deer, looking in my direction. Buck or doe? It was the size of the former, but no horns were visible in those shadows. I stood and stood and waited. So did that deer.

Experience told me just what would happen, but I would have to prove it— there was one chance in ten. Some hunters would have fired and then gone down to look for horns. I am not that kind. So, slowly with the persistence of a snail, I removed myself from the gaze of the foe and then quickly circled down to command the spot. It was empty!

Once more I had proved that when you are once in the eye of a deer, you should stay there. He has more patience than you have, but the moment you hide from him he will break away. And now, as it seemed not my lucky day, I took out my compass and headed trailward, seeing nothing en route except a little fellow I jumped out of a bed below a hemlock thicket.

There was only one thing to do about it, and a hunter is a hopeful creature. To find that big "moose of a deer" up Dove Creek among all those trees might be a needle-in-the-haystack game. Yet I was sure he was waiting for me there somewhere.

Daylight again saw me on tiptoe boring off into the shadows from the low ridge where the blazes did their fade-out, but today I planned to hunt lower. By algebra, geometry, trigonometry and plain horse sense I had proved, theoretically at least, that these bucks were coy, using the salal ridges merely as feeding, fighting and courting grounds and hiding out by day down in the thickets. They preferred whole and unpunctured skins, life and love to ultra-violet rays.

In half an hour of pussy-footing in the silences, where often I could hear my heart beat as I stood to read the shadows in eyeshot, I thought I had proved my case. There, before me, with his head down, was a little deer—a spiker. When he lifted his head in that sudden snappy way of a deer, he saw me instantly. As usual I wore my crimson shirt—I wear this, of course, in hope that at sight of it a deer will be more interested in me, and other hunters less—and in wide astonishment the little fellow froze and stared.

"Well! Some gaudy forest flower!" I could see the thought in his pop-eyed countenance.

He was approaching, coming with sudden mincing steps, stiff-legged. Yards became feet, yet I moved not a muscle. With half-closed eyes, so that he could not see me wink, I tried to breathe without movement. At ten feet there was a big fir in the way, and he stole around and peeped at me comically. This was almost too much for me.

Just when I was wondering if a wild deer ever ate the lunch out of a hunter's pocket, he got a whiff of the man scent. Sudden understanding, disgust and consternation swept over that little buck, and his legs did their duty. He grew more scared with every jump as he went down the slope.

After this I was prepared for anything. Before long, as I stole down a slight hogback thickly grown with young hemlocks whose dead lower limbs allowed the eye to penetrate a little, I saw a big shadowy form that made my heart skip a beat. No spiker that, but a grandpap. However, even at twenty-five yards I could make out only dimly the gray outline, and no horns were visible.

Broadside, with head turned staring at me, he was absolutely motionless. His eye had caught my movement. A windfallen log covered most of his body. His shoulder was hidden by two small trees

A majestic buck bedded down in a field near Boulder, Colorado. (Photo © Michael Mauro)

Above: *If it weren't for such bodacious ears, these does could have remained unseen in their tallgrass prairie beds. (Photo © Michael Mauro)*
Facing page: *Alaska's Tongass National Forest, which stretches over much of southeast Alaska, harbors the tiny Sitka blacktail. Throughout their range, they coexist relatively peacefully with grizzly bears. (Photo © Erwin and Peggy Bauer)*

and his face screened behind branches, so that I could not swear to the gray telltale nose of the buck; but I could see his white throat patch plainly. A buck, yes; but strain my eyes as I might, I could see no sign of horns.

Inch by inch I raised my rifle and covered the dim form. I knew he must turn his head before he moved and in that instant I would see his horns; but this deer might have been carved in granite. My arms began to ache, and I had to lower my rifle. And at that instant he moved—he did a sudden eyes right, and in one motion bounded forward through that five-foot gap of visibility. Horns! I saw them then, all right. I had been looking too low. There was no time for sights. Firing by feel and instinct, I listened to hear him fall.

There was not a sound. I had not even heard him land from that mighty bound. He was a phantom. Not a hoof-print, not a hair, no drop of blood could I find on the needles.

Had I been dreaming? No, there was my empty shell. Now I took the line of fire, and there it was! My bullet had slammed into the side of a ten-inch hemlock. Well, the elevation was right anyhow—but no luck could retrieve such a day, and I went home with my head full of that big buck and speculating on when I would be able to do something right.

The high ridge, with its sunny slope toward the chattering creek, drew me now as a magnet draws a needle. That biggest one was still up there—somewhere. When next, on a sunny morning, I left the blind trail, I took a new course, holding more to the creek side but there was less sign of the elusive blacktail here. About ten o'clock I could see, looming against the skyline, the nose of a ridge that I judged the highest one.

I was early. Pausing at the base of the slope, I explored its sunny patches and dark shadows among the firs and cedars above me. What place more fitting for Mowitch to take a siesta? Why could not that "moose of a deer" be there now as reward for the miles and miles I had tiptoed through these green woods?

I started up the hill, and then my heart gave a bound. A deer was running along the slope, flashing in and out of the sun as he turned the shoulder. He appeared to be a little fellow, and I had about lost interest in him when he did something which stirred me anew. Pausing at the turn and standing screened by a clump of low cedars, he raised and lowered his head two or three times—an action I had never seen from other than an old buck.

He was not badly frightened—had probably glimpsed my red shirt. I had the wind; he could not see me now, I knew. So, stealing back, I circled away up over the back of the ridge, gave him half an hour to forget me and worked with the caution of a cat out to the sunny brow about four hundred yards ahead. And there he was, right under my nose—twenty-five yards away. The deer I had been looking for!

Those long prongs, glinting in the sun, gave me a thrill I had never felt in these woods. He saw me on the instant and dashing off, vanished in two jumps; but there was a clean gap he must cross, and to the crack of my .250 he dropped.

There he lay in the sun-warmed salal, the finest old stag I had yet seen in Vancouver Island woods. Perfect in every one of his ten points, with a 19-inch spread—a sight to bring the satisfaction that only a hunter can quite know. And when I turned him over, there, across his back, was a little cut where a bullet had formerly slit the skin: the trade-mark of one Cougar Smith.

Two hours later, struggling under my burden—145 pounds dressed out—I came out upon the pack trail. When you are tip-toeing in the tall timber after blacktails, you may get that big one if your toes hold out.

Facing page: *Mature muley bucks reach maximum antler growth between five and a half and six and a half years of age. (Photo © D. Robert Franz)*
Overleaf: *This blacktail deer calls Oregon's Willamette River valley home. (Photo © Michael Wilhelm/ENP Images)*

THE BIG BUCK OF
THE BEAR CREEK BURNS

by Elliott S. Barker

Elliott S. Barker began his career in the outdoors in 1907 as a professional guide and hunter near Las Vegas, New Mexico. He later joined the U.S. Forest Service and worked as a forest ranger and then as a forest supervisor on federal lands in New Mexico. After a stint as a rancher, he became New Mexico's first state game warden in 1931, directing the Department of Game and Fish until his retirement twenty-two years later.

Barker's writing appeared in *Outdoor Life*, *Field & Stream*, *American Forests*, and other national magazines, and he also published several books on outdoors subjects, including *When the Dogs Barked "Treed": A Year on the Trail of the Longtails* and *Eighty Years with Rod and Rifle*. The "Big Buck of the Bear Creek Burns" originally appeared in his 1953 book *Beatty's Cabin: Adventures in the Pecos High Country*. Barker's story describes the pursuit of a majestic buck from a unique viewpoint: that of the deer itself.

The big, old mule deer buck spent the night alone in a little glade at the head of Beaver Creek in the high Sangre de Cristo Range. It was a bitter cold, frosty night. The forest, through which distant rifle shots had echoed during the day, was now silent and peaceful.

The big buck had made his supper on the dried leaves and seed pods of such palatable plants as protruded through the snow, and had nuzzled down around the stalks for the tenderer leaves buried beneath it. When he had finished, he had drunk from the little spring that gurgles out of the steep hillside from beneath a boulder. He then had made his bed in the snow, sheltered by the drooping branches of a big spruce tree.

At the first pale light of dawn, the big buck left his snowy bed and set out across the divide westward toward the Bear Creek burns. The evergreen forest was painted sparkling gray, with frozen moisture clinging to every branch and needle. The leaves of brush and herbs alike that he selected for his breakfast as he went along, were gilded with crisp frost crystals.

All summer long the big buck had ranged alone, or with other bucks in the seclusion of the remote forest, while fattening and growing his new set of antlers. His antlers were now full grown and their summer covering of live, velvety skin had dried and been rubbed off. It was a nice set of widespread, long, pointed antlers, and the old buck was proud of them.

A spectacular buck in an early fall snowfall. (Photo © Brad Garfield)

No longer was the old fellow content to be alone. He had become restless, craving company; and the feminine companionship which had been shunned all summer and fall had become a necessity. Love season was now at hand and his whole being had suddenly become tuned up to a high pitch in anticipation of the thrills of combat with rivals, and the rewards of victory over them. He had already tarried too long alone in the deep forest, awaiting the end of the hunting season, but now he determined to find quickly, and appropriate for himself, a band of sleek, mild-eyed does.

He chose the Bear Creek burns not only because he knew there were some bands of beautiful does there, but also because, this late in the season, there would likely be no hunters in that remote, isolated area. He knew well there would be some big, stout bucks, with massive antlers, to overcome. Then, too, there would be young whippersnappers, not bold enough to engage in decisive combat, who would pester him constantly by seizing every opportunity to mingle for a brief moment with the band.

But the buck with the long, widespread antlers was big, fat, and strong, and well experienced in the use of his stout, sharp-pointed weapons. Not a tremor of fear entered his strong heart; instead, the hot blood in his veins coursed with self-confidence, and his muscles flexed with energy. His whole being was fired and his nerves tingled with zest for the seasonal ceremonies that lay ahead. He bowed his already enlarged neck and proudly determined to take on, in mortal combat, any buck who dared challenge his intention to father a goodly number of next year's fawns.

The first pink rays of the morning sun had brought sparkling light and life to the dark, silent forest, as the big, longhorned buck stepped boldly out of the log-strewn, open strip that extends eastward from the head of Bear Creek. Already, the welcome scent of a band of deer had reached his keen nostrils, and he set out in a brisk walk in the direction of the herd. At the point of timber where the big burned area, strewn with bleached and rotting logs, opened out ahead of him, he saw a beautiful band of does feeding quietly on cinquefoil sticking up through the crusted snow. It was a beautiful, gratifying sight—a sight that charged the old, enamored buck through and through with desire and determination. With antlers held high, the big buck trotted proudly and boldly out toward the lovely creatures, who quickly raised their shapely heads to watch his approach.

What a find it was, nine lithe, soft-eyed does, ripe for courtship and not another buck in sight! When he came near to the band, a two-year-old doe came forward to greet him, stepping high and cautiously, her big, well-formed ears thrown forward and her head swaying slightly up and down with each graceful step. The big buck and young doe touched noses lightly, then tentatively touched noses to flanks. An old doe came forward and jealously butted the young lady away.

Then suddenly, as there came to his ears the sound of intermittent clashing of antlers, the old buck's body tensed and he bowed his thick neck for combat. Already, tentatively two bucks were contesting for supremacy and the right to squire this choice band of does during the ensuing weeks.

The rattling and clashing of antlers ceased, and, in a moment, a lordly fellow with massive antlers walked proudly toward the herd, followed at a safe distance by another fine, sleek, young buck. The lordly one came boldly on. Then, with equal boldness and determination born of intense, jealous desire, the old, long-horned buck stepped out between him and the band of does to challenge his right to join it. The lordly fellow, already in a fighting mood, promptly accepted the challenge. The ladies turned to watch while the third buck stood by, waiting to seize the advantage by taking on the tired victor.

The two big mule deer approached each other cautiously, with lowered heads turned slightly to one side, necks bowed, and every sinew in their bodies tense. When three lengths apart, they paused, alert and ready for the charge. At some mysterious signal understood by both, they plunged together, head-on, with a terrific, brain-jarring clash of antlers. Neither one gave any ground; but stood and fought for a moment, toe to toe, with a noisy rattling of tines, each seeking a chance to slip past the other's rack

A muley in North Dakota's badlands. Lewis and Clark first identified mule deer in 1804 while traveling up the Missouri River not far from this region. (Photo © Michael H. Francis)

and plunge sharp points into the ribs of his adversary.

Then, by mutual consent, they backed off again, three lengths apart, and again rushed together, with a stunning impact, and sparred for an opening to reach shoulder, ribs, or flank. Then, all at once, the band of does and fawns whirled and bounded off in terrified flight over the bleached logs, toward the brink of the hill. That could mean but one thing—they had detected a deadly enemy approaching, a lion or a hunter. Forgetting their hatred for each other, the combatants backed away, instantly alert for scent, sight, or sound of the common enemy.

A hundred yards away, just barely in time, they saw a red-capped hunter pull his rifle from the saddle scabbard and hurriedly get off his horse. The old buck wheeled and bounded off at top speed over the logs toward a patch of spruce timber two hundred yards away, to the left of where the does had gone. His formidable, erstwhile antagonists cut back to the right of the does, where scattering second-growth fir and spruce afforded some cover.

Three quick shots were fired at the two bucks, as they raced for their lives, but the bullets passed harmlessly behind them. Then the hunter swung around and fired at the old, long-horned buck just as he entered the timber, the bullet passing over his back much too close for comfort.

The old fellow swung to the right, keeping in the timber for a quarter mile. Then he slowly came out to the edge of an open, rocky knoll from where, well camouflaged, he could look back and see what the hunter was doing. The hunter tied his horse to a sapling and followed the tracks of the two bucks as if he expected them to stop there in the open area, as indeed they sometimes do when separated from a band. As the old, long-horned buck watched, he felt perfectly safe, but dared not go back to his beloved does for to do so might endanger them as well as himself.

The old buck watched the hunter as he moved forward slowly and carefully. He also watched the other bucks as they turned up the hill at right angles to their back tracks for a hundred yards or so, then came back parallel to them a short distance, where they took up vigil, peeking through the branches of some young fir trees. The cautious, red-capped hunter crunched along, watching straight ahead with rifle ready. When the hunter cautiously came along

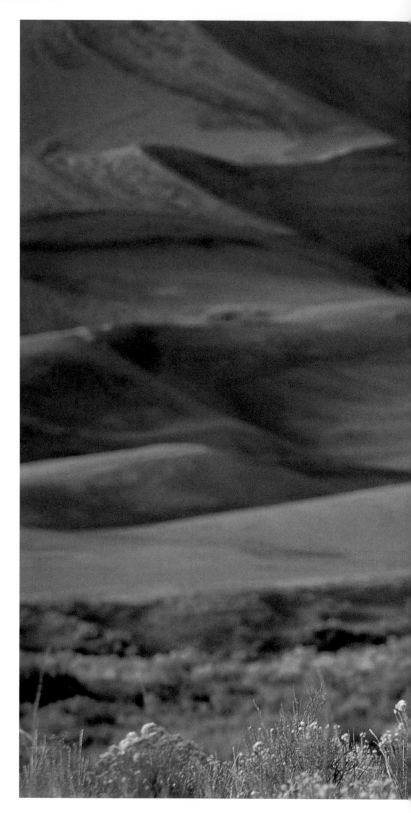

A doe in autumn light on the edge of Colorado's Great Sand Dunes National Monument. (Photo © Henry H. Holdsworth/Wild By Nature)

The Boone and Crockett Club, founded in 1887 by Theodore Roosevelt to emphasize the conservation of critical habitat and the principle of fair chase, has greatly aided mule deer by lobbying for the establishment of national parks, forests, and wildlife refuges all over the American West. (Photo © Alan and Sandy Carey)

A big rack is the result of genetics and excellent nutrition—majesty runs in the family, as long as the healthy parents' offspring has plenty of nourishing browse. (Photo © James Prout)

opposite the hiding place of the two bucks, they snorted contemptuously and bounded away out of sight. The hunter was so startled he nearly dropped his rifle and, before he could recover his senses, the bucks were safely out of sight. The nimrod brushed the snow off a log and sat down disgustedly. There he waited a long time wishing, without hope, that a buck would be silly enough to come within sight and range. Meanwhile, the long-horned buck moved to a more secluded spot and bedded down and waited patiently.

Finally, the hunter went back, got on his horse, and followed the big old buck's tracks across the burn and into the timber. The wise old fellow could hear the hunter coming toward him and, to fool him, got up and walked briskly on around the hillside for a little way, then circled in a trot up the hill, and then back to a spot from which he could see his bed without being seen. When the hunter came to the bed, he dismounted and looked longingly in the direction the buck had gone when he left the spot. At that instant Old Long Horns, from his vantage point up the hill, blew him a good-by, whistling snort, and bounded away through the timber. He ran a couple of hundred yards up the steep hill, then stopped to listen. The horse made so much noise clambering over rocks and breaking dead limbs as he climbed the hill, that the buck could tell just where the hunter was at all times. The buck walked to the left, around the hillside for a short distance, then turned back down the hill to his own tracks and those of the horse, which he followed back to his old bed. From there, he continued on in the horse tracks up the hill when he heard the hunter coming along. Who was chasing whom, anyway?

As the buck went around the circle for the second time, often stepping right in the horse's tracks, he could hear the noisy hunter and kept well ahead of him. Then, as he approached his old bed, the noise stopped and he felt sure his tormentor had abandoned the chase. To verify that, the old fellow started on to his original lookout point, to watch for the hunter to see if he crossed the burn.

Suddenly he froze in his tracks. There at his old bed, through the trees, he could indistinctly see the hunter's black horse. The hunter had left his horse

there, and had followed on afoot, very noisily for awhile, to make the buck think he was still horseback. Then he had become quiet to make the buck think he had given up the chase.

Now the old buck listened intently, but no sound came to him. He sniffed the air repeatedly, but it was so pervaded with horse and man scent that he could not locate the hunter, though he knew he must be near. But where? The danger of this trick was not new to the wise old buck, but he had fallen for it and now found himself in deadly peril. Hastily, he decided that safety for him lay in flight right up the hill.

Slowly he turned that way, then stopped. All at once, a hundred yards straight up the hill, the excited chattering of a chickaree squirrel burst out in the silent forest. That told the old buck that the hunter had just passed under his nest tree. The timely warning from his little friend is all that saved the buck from stopping some hot lead. Quickly he turned and bounded around the hillside out of that perilous trap to safety.

Old Long Horns had successfully eluded many a hunter before, and, even though this one was no novice, he felt that he could outsmart him, too. So he ran on to the point of timber from where he had seen the does at sunrise. From safe cover in the deep shadow of the timber, the buck watched his back track and listened intently. After awhile he heard the horse and glimpsed horse and rider coming out into the neck of the burn. Cautiously, he eased back into the forest, then made tracks as fast as he could back toward Beaver Creek. For a quarter mile he kept under cover, then deliberately went out into the open strip of the burn for a hundred yards or so, as if to cross it. Then he turned back sharply into the edge of the timber and followed it for fifty steps. There he lay down behind a log, with some dead limbs sticking up, to watch his back track.

After awhile the determined hunter, now afoot, came on slowly and cautiously. He followed the tracks out into the open area, thinking the buck had crossed it. But this time, he stopped often and looked in all directions, even straight at the buck's hiding place, but did not see him, so well was he concealed behind the log with the brushy dead limbs.

A thick-necked buck in the midst of the November rut. (Photo © Michael H. Francis)

Above: *The thick-beamed, towering antlers of this Rocky Mountain buck seem almost unwieldy. (Photo © D. Robert Franz)*
Facing page: *An estimated three million mule and blacktailed deer range across western North America. (Photo © D. Robert Franz)*
Overleaf: *Though bucks and does naturally come together during the rutting season, they tend to keep their distance from each other much of the rest of the year. (Photo © Michael H. Francis)*

When the hunter looked the other way, the buck leaped from his bed and beat it like a flash into the dense timber, out of sight. The hunter, hearing a twig snap, turned quickly, just in time to glimpse a white rump as it disappeared in tile timber, but not in time to shoot. Even as he fled, the buck's keen ears caught the sound of the hunter cursing his own carelessness.

While the buck ran at top speed for three hundred yards to make his tormentor think he was really leaving the country this time, he stopped as suddenly as he had started. Right there he turned around and, peeking through the branches of some little fir trees, began again to watch his back track. For awhile he heard the chattering of a chickaree squirrel who had been startled when the buck leaped from his bed. Then all was quiet except for the murmuring of the gentle breeze in the treetops. He waited, motionless, for a long time but no sound of the hunter came, and the wind had switched around so that he could not scent him either.

Finally, he lay down and continued to look, listen, and sniff. A snowshoe rabbit passed close by but didn't see him. Later a pair of Canadian jays perched on limbs within a few feet and made a close inspection. At last, after much bird whistle-talk, their curiosity satisfied, they flew away.

The sun was away past meridian when the patient old fellow, believing the chase had been abandoned by the hunter, got up, stretched his slender legs, and walked on slowly, still intensively alert, toward the familiar Beaver Creek area. When near the top of the range, the buck skirted the edge of a long glade and stopped at the opposite end of it, where, shielded from view by a newly wind-thrown fir, he could see quite a way back along his track.

He listened intently for the warning chatter of

his little squirrel friends, but heard nothing. As the long minutes passed, it seemed more and more certain that he would be bothered no more by the pesky, red-capped hunter. Yet, though the temptation was strong, he dared not go back to find his harem, until dusk.

Well past mid-afternoon he gave up his vigil and moved on to the east side of the range. Slowly he worked his way down the steep, timbered slope, still alert. He remembered a brush patch around the hillside a half mile or so away. There would be a good place to while away the time, feeding on leaves and tender twigs, for now he was hungry. While feeding, his thoughts turned again to the seasonal necessity for feminine companionship.

The old, long-horned buck's blood once more was warming and his nerves tingling with desire and anticipation. He also thought of those other big stout bucks whom he would have to fight and defeat decisively in order to claim his ladies. Just to prove to himself how ready for combat he really was, he started horning a fir sapling and quickly stripped it of bark and limbs. The valiant old fellow's fighting spirit was being tuned up to a high pitch as he turned from one little fir to another, horning them vigorously, demonstrating how quickly he would trim those other bucks.

Then he heard a twig crack, then the faint crunch of snow not fifty paces away. Instantly, the big buck realized that in his mock battle, he had become inexcusably careless. The persistent, red-capped hunter had waited long and patiently, then followed on. He was right there, had heard the buck, knew exactly where he was, but because of a clump of bushes, could not see him.

Instantly appraising the desperate situation, the big buck whirled around and dashed recklessly at top speed right down the hill. A few big jumps put him in the timber without being seen, and, he thought, permanently out of sight. He could not know that there was a little alley-like opening through the trees which he would have to cross and in which, seventy paces away, the hunter was standing, alert and ready.

As he crossed that narrow open space through the trees, almost in a single bound, out of the corner of his eye he glimpsed the red-capped hunter with rifle leveled. He saw a flash, heard the sharp report of the rifle, and felt a terrible shock in his loins and back. The big, long-horned buck skidded and landed with his body out of control. His back was broken and his hind quarters paralyzed. Struggling upright on his front feet, he dragged his hind quarters on down the hill to a little flat place above a dense clump of trees, and lay down, his hind legs sticking out awkwardly. He realized he was finished and that he would never get back to the Bear Creek burns to assert his right to court and caress those precious does. All the same, if his despised tormentor should come within reach, he was determined to rip him to pieces with sharp tines and front feet in spite of a broken back.

Now the sportsman was coming down the hill toward his helpless quarry, for which he had worked hard and patiently. He came slowly, cautiously, with rifle ready, not knowing how badly he had disabled the big buck. As he came in sight forty paces away, the old buck's body tensed; but he made no effort to move. They watched each other briefly. Slowly the sportsman leveled his deadly rifle for the mercy shot. As the old long-horned buck waited, there was a flash, a deafening report, and all went dark—but he felt nothing.

Muley and whitetailed deer ranges overlap throughout the West, though they have distinctive habitats. Whitetails prefer the forests whereas muleys tend to favor mountainous terrain and the wide-open plains. (Photo © Sherm Spoelstra)

Chapter 4

MAJESTIC MULE DEER

*"A fine specimen of a blacktailed deer went bounding past camp
this morning. A buck with wide spread of antlers, showing admirable
vigor and grace. . . . Every motion and posture is graceful, the
very poetry of manners and motion. . . ."*
—John Muir, My First Summer in the Sierra, 1916

WHITE SADDLE BUCK

by Rutherford G. Montgomery

Mule deer share their range with spectacular animals: elk, wolves, grizzlies, pronghorn, moose. They certainly have ears that would make a Grand Canyon pack mule green with envy. But any hunter who has stumbled across a mighty buck on a ridge as the sun rises to begin a new hunting season, any hunter who has pushed on through brambles, over mountains, up and down gulches, and through snowdrifts, knows and believes there is only one animal out there: the majestic mule deer.

Rutherford G. Montgomery lived a remarkable life, and in fact didn't discover his talent for writing until he was forty-five. He began his career as a teacher and soon became a principal, but left education after a few years to serve as a county judge in Colorado. He later assumed the post of Colorado state budget commissioner, but resigned that position after six years to pursue freelance writing full time.

Known primarily for his fiction for children, including more than eighty books for kids, Montgomery also published six novels, many about western ranching issues; served as a ghost writer for the Dick Tracy comic strip series; and wrote screenplays, including work he completed during a four-year stay at the Walt Disney Company. "White Saddle Buck" appeared in Montgomery's *High Country*, a fictional account of the adventures of a quirky hunting party pursuing big game in the Colorado mountains.

F all haze hung like a translucent purple veil over the high country. The clear dustless air held a tang of earthy smells which mingled with the spice of balsam, spruce and hemlock. Drawn deep into the lungs, it invigorated and rejuvenated. The aspen belt was aflame with yellow, solid color varying only at the tops of stray trees where it merged into scarlet. Below Wind Ridge the valley of the Big Blue drowsed in the late afternoon sun of an Indian-summer day. Above the ridge towered the white peaks of Gold Mountain.

Tex, the horse wrangler, shoved his floppy hat far back on his head and squinted at the scene below. His eyes, used to looking far through thin air, noted the canyons and trails

Pages 118–119, main photo: *Mule deer are the venerable trophy deer of the North American West. (Photo © Michael H. Francis)*

Page 119, inset: *Idahoan Stanley Easton poses with his game. Circa 1927. (Photo courtesy Idaho State Historical Society, #P1996.25.22.)*

Facing page: *A spectacular buck on a Colorado mountainside. (Photo © D. Robert Franz)*

leading to the valley. His half-broken, blue-black bronc shook his bridle impatiently and dug deep into the black turf.

Ranged beside Tex, bending over stock saddles, sat the Governor on a rangy white gelding, silent under the spell of the barrens; Bill on a sleepy bay; Doc lazily chewing a twig, giving his big sorrel his head to allow him freedom to crop the ripe grass; the Sheriff astride a lean roan; and Dave on a pie-bald with an uncertain glass eye. Below a six-horse pack outfit sat Hopi Joe, bare to his waist, his copper skin gleaming in the sunlight, his feet pulled up on the bare back of a mouse-grey pony. Hopi Joe was staring unwinking up at the white reaches of Gold Mountain.

"We'll bed down along the trail any time you say." Tex addressed the Governor.

"Water and wood, son." The Governor shoved back his wide hat and eased his sore joints in the saddle.

"From daylight on." Tex grinned. "Mighty long trail for a tenderfoot."

"Ask Bill." The Governor pulled out his field-glasses and gave his attention to a distant ridge.

"You ducks can't scare me out. Tomorrow I'll rest while you beat the bushes for meat and wear blisters on your pelts. Fact is, I'm beginning to rest the minute we hit camp." Bill's big nose and shaggy brows gave him a fierce expression. His ample paunch sagged over the roll of the saddle allowing a massive gold chain and fob to dangle over the horn.

Doc and the Sheriff said nothing. Doc never admitted fatigue. He drank bicarbonate of soda and water when his stomach knotted, reminding him it was a poor organ to abuse, and went on with the gang. The Sheriff was in the saddle almost daily and hardened to it. A few hours more would not worry or tire him.

"Camp it is, just beyond that clump of spruce." Tex waved his hand and whistled shrilly.

Hopi Joe half turned and answered Tex's signal, then clucked to the mouse-gray pony. The pack-horses stirred and shook their heads. Slowly the out-fit moved up the trail.

A big-bodied buck with a wide rack. (Photo © Michael Mauro)

Above: *Mule deer are as much a part of the stunning lands of the North American West as the mountains. (Photo © Henry H. Holdsworth/Wild By Nature)*
Facing page: *Mule deer bucks shed their antlers between January and March; a new set begins growth in March or April. This buck, bedding down in late summer, sports a velvety rack with impressive growth. (Photo © Michael Mauro)*

Tex halted the outfit at the edge of a little meadow through which a clear stream wandered. As the pack outfit arrived and closed around the wrangler the Governor laughed eagerly.

"Boy, this is great!" He leaned back and breathed deeply.

From the spruce above, a two-point buck broke cover and trotted across the meadow. The Governor pulled out his .30-06 and slid the bolt back. Holding the front bead on the moving shoulder of the buck, he watched the trim monarch flash his white backside at the party and disappear into the timber.

"No score on anything except timberline buck!" Doc sang out.

"What a target!" The Governor lowered his .30-06 and slid it back into its saddle scabbard.

"You won't get any cracks like that at a timberline buck," the Sheriff warned. "You should have cracked down on that baby and saved yourself from a skunking."

"Nothing less than top score goes for me." The Governor slid stiffly from his saddle and bent a broad shoulder against the white gelding. One jerk loosened the girth and he tossed the saddle and blanket to the grass, up-ending it neatly.

"I always take a nip along about this time," Bill announced.

Rattling in the grub box he got out a tin cup and blew in it to remove the oat dust and horsehairs. With a flourish he poured a stiff drink from his saddle flask.

"Anyone joining me has to get their own cup," he said.

The Governor held up a cup of water from the cold stream. Doc produced a flask filled with a thick solution of bicarbonate of soda and water. With a

Above: *The blacktail has a distinctive, nearly all-black tail. (Photo © Jeffrey Rich)*
Left: *A lordly buck in the foggy foothills. (Photo © Mark and Jennifer Miller)*

show of dignity he poured himself a drink. The Sheriff and Dave got cups and held them while Bill poured their drinks. Tex, suddenly breaking away from his horse, approached and sniffed eagerly.

"Don't mind if I do," he said as he reached for a tin cup. Bill poured him a drink and Tex, after removing a glove, began fishing horsehairs out of it with a stubby finger.

The cups were raised in a circle. Hopi Joe stood aside watching with a sombre face.

"Timberline buck!" The toast was in unison.

"I read in the public press about a duel between the Governor of Colorado and a sheriff. No meat except with a .38 special, six-inch barrel." Bill was grinning like a wrinkled, fat Chinese god. He had his eye on Hopi Joe. It would be fine if the Indian would offer to unsaddle his horse.

"Right as one of your famous election predictions, Bill." The Governor was untangling a pair of hobbles from a bunch tied to one of the pack saddles. "Six-guns get the first inning but I'm taking along my .30-06. I aim to bag a timberline buck."

The Sheriff grinned widely. "Keep that alibi in mind, boys," he said as he stripped his saddle off the roan.

Doc removed his saddle and stacked it, then jumped up and down slapping his elk-hide chaps with his old hat and yipping cowboy fashion, "Ride 'em, cowboy!"

Bill moved toward his horse. Hopi Joe was busy with the pack string. With a deep sigh he jerked on the cinch strap. His horse grunted and moved away from him but the strap loosened and Bill pulled the saddle over the placid bay's flanks.

Presently Hopi Joe turned to gathering wood for the fire and piling it beside two big granite boulders. Tex whistled in a monotone as he cared for the horses. Bill seated himself on a flat stone and got out a blackened briar pipe while the others set about making camp.

Soon Hopi Joe had a fire roaring. Dave and the Sheriff strung up a tarp for a windbreak while Doc and the Governor got out pots and pans and a big, black coffeepot. Bill watched them speculatively. When they lifted out the tinware and did not return

to the pack again he got stiffly to his feet and shuffled over to one of the panyards. Rummaging about, he fished out a brown quart bottle and placed it on his bed-roll.

"Water and wood and camp." Dave Walters spoke with a wide, tired grin. Being chief executive of a steel mill close to sea level was poor training for a hard saddle jaunt at nine thousand feet in the thin Colorado air.

The men turned to the packs and got out blankets and sheep-lined coats. Seating themselves beside the fire, they lighted pipes or cigarettes while Tex set out the Dutch oven and raked coals from the fire to bank it with.

Long shadows crept out of the spruce and stretched across the tall-grass meadow. Two does with fawns mincing ahead of them slid out of the timber and moved toward the cold stream. They advanced a few yards, stopped with their big ears cocked forward, then moved again. When they stopped, their grey buck color blended with the frost-dead grass. Quickly the chill air from the snows above timberline settled along the slope, and the men pulled their heavy coats closer around them. The does halted beside the cold stream, thrusting their noses deep into the icy water and blowing lustily. From the upper end of the meadow came the mellow notes of the jingle-horse's bell. Far to the south a coyote called, long and mournfully.

Beside the fire the men were loath to break the spell which had descended with the coming of dusk. Mingled with the vastness of the high country was a lonely stillness which only the wild things seemed privileged to shatter.

The Governor sniffed hungrily, his eyes following Tex who was busily working beside a small fire he had drawn from the log blaze. Tex had just clapped the lid on the Dutch oven. In the deep hog-lard within rested row upon row of fat, fast-rising biscuits. The coffee suddenly came to a boil and Tex dashed a cup of cold water into the pot, then pulled it back from the fire, but not before a streak of brown grounds had dripped down along the spout. A rich odor arose from the pot.

"This is punishment," Bill rumbled as he stuffed

Unlike a whitetail rack, which has tines extending from main beams, mature mule and blacktailed deer antlers have multiple forks. (Photo © Bruce Montagne)

more rough-cut into his briar and sniffed noisily.

Bacon strips, brown and curling, cut thick by Tex's hunting knife, began to pile high on a tin plate close to the fire. The skillet smoked as Tex dropped more thick strips into the sizzling grease. Tex set out a wooden pail of honey and one of strawberry jam. An instant later he was ploughing a wooden spoon through a heaping skillet of browning potatoes. Straightening, he mopped his forehead. A peek into the Dutch oven and he turned to the men beside the fire.

"Come and get it!"

There was a hurried rush of boots as the hungry party swarmed around the food. Tin plates were piled high and striped with rows of browned biscuits. Black coffee, and coffee with tinned cream and sugar from a pail was set out to cool. Each returned to his seat and attacked the food. Doc avoided the fried potatoes but filled his plate with biscuit and bacon. After the men had seated themselves Hopi Joe appeared out of the dusk. He stood smiling upon the men.

"If you hunt so well," he said softly.

"Grab a platter and get in." Tex waved a biscuit dripping with honey.

Hopi Joe got a plate and filled it. Squatting beside the fire he gave his undivided attention to the bacon, fried potatoes, biscuits and black unsweetened coffee.

The Governor finished the last biscuit, breaking it and sopping it in bacon grease. He rubbed his belly and let his heavy belt out a notch.

"Why does anyone want to be Governor of Colorado?" He sank beside the fire.

"I've a notion to stay," Dave said as he locked his hands behind his head and lay back.

Tom and the Sheriff were scraping their plates and washing them in a pot of hot water Tex had pulled back from the fire. Reluctantly the others got up and washed their dishes. Bill grunted and had to take a small nip from the Bourbon bottle before he could get to this last chore of the evening.

Beyond the arching yellow sweep of the campfire the stars gleamed big and white, like icy jewels. Through the thin air they seemed close above the camp.

Pipes were soon drawing evenly as the wavering light from the fire played over the circle of faces. The Governor's was relaxed and peaceful, but tired lines showed plainly, lines written on his forehead by worry and constant tension. Dave's chin already showed a blue stubble which stood out against the untanned whiteness of his face. Dave had a powerful chin and dark, direct eyes. Even in repose there was a restless strength about him. The Sheriff was wind-tanned with a smooth, leathery face and eyes used to looking out over vast valleys and broken ridges—steady eyes, undisturbed and calm. Doc's lean face carried the marks of his long struggle for health, the taut leanness of a man who had cheated death by a close margin. Tex sat bow-legged, his high heels together, his weather-roughened face bent toward the fire, a smoking cigarette hanging from his lips. Bill had found a stump to rest against and his face was in the shadow. A red glow showed through the gloom as he pulled on his pipe. Hopi Joe sat beside the cook fire, apart from the others. He had a light jacket pulled around his shoulders and his finely molded profile looked like a master's bronze.

"I figure to get the white-saddle buck this fall," Doc said softly.

"Not if I get the chance I muffed last fall," the Sheriff grinned. "He broke out of a tangle of down timber, doubled like a wild hoss, and shot over a cut bank and into Beaver Canyon."

"Got to be smarter than the buck," Bill observed.

"He'll be dyin' of old age if you don't bring him down pretty soon," Tex laughed. "What is this? Five falls we've heard about a white-saddle buck."

"You can pack him in for me this fall, Tex," the Governor said.

"I've had him cornered twice up at the head of Wind Ridge. He always vanishes into thin air." Dave spoke slowly. "This year I'm coming up from the north."

Hopi Joe looked up from his meditation but said nothing. He, too, had seen the white-saddle buck, a big timberline monarch, rugged and powerful, marked by a freak saddle of white just back of his shoulders. Hopi Joe was close to the witchcraft of the woods and had a conviction the white-saddle buck was no ordinary mule deer. He would not be

Mule deer sport a reddish brown coat during summer; over winter, a heavier, better-insulated, grayish brown coat develops. (Photo © Sherm Spoelstra)

Above: *Mule deer country: Gunnison National Forest, Colorado. (Photo © Sherm Spoelstra)*
Right: *Mule deer does in early winter. (Photo © Michael Quinton)*

killed by a rifle bullet—Hopi Joe was certain of that. He was certain because he had stood silent beside a spruce for eight hours waiting for a shot at the big fellow. When the chance came Hopi Joe had over-shot a clean foot. He had discovered his rear sight was jacked up, possibly by a thorn bush, but that had not altered his conclusion. The white-saddle buck was not marked for a bullet.

"Is it rifles on the white-saddle buck?" the Sher-iff asked of the Governor.

"We'll make that the one exception," the Gover-nor agreed.

Doc got to his feet and ground out his cigarette with a boot heel. Silhouetted against the night he looked like a slat frame upon which hunting togs had been draped.

"The old wind mattress will feel good tonight," he said as he set about getting his sleeping bag ready.

The others joined him and soon a row of wool socks hung from a limb beside the fire with boots lined under them. Bed-roll flaps were pulled snugly over the heads of the hunters and silence claimed the camp. Tex stayed up to have a look at the horses. The others were sleeping soundly when he returned to the dying fire and jerked off his worn boots. For an-other half-hour he sat with his sock-feet extended to the heat, and smoked.

A great party, this group of men who came with him every fall into the roughest of western Colorado mountains. Take the Governor—he loved the moun-tains, the hard riding over rough trails—not bad with a rope, either—should have been a cattleman. He was strong, of tough fiber, able to take in his stride the demands of the yellow press that he commute the sentence of a murderer of two little girls. Tex knew he would not commute the sentence, although the decision would not be made until after the hunt.

Then there was Doc—fighting a desperate battle against stomach ulcers. Tough as any of the gang, always in good humor even when drinking a thick solution of baking soda and water. And Dave who ruled a veritable kingdom and whose word was law in a hundred offices and a dozen great mills. A real trail-man after his seat toughened and his knees loos-ened to fit the saddle. The Sheriff, of course, was his

own kind, brother of the big outdoors, a cowboy at fifteen and on his own on a Wyoming ranch.

Hopi Joe broke in on his thoughts. The Indian appeared out of the night and seated himself beside Tex.

"You're like a dratted haunt," Tex muttered.

"The deer still feed high," Hopi Joe said softly.

Tex nodded. "Say, Joe," he asked, "why don't you ever kill a buck when we come hunting? "

"There is no need. I kill for food. Once I would kill the white-saddle buck but he is marked by the Great Spirit so I cannot kill him either." Hopi Joe stared into the embers of the fire.

"But you always come along?" Tex was curious.

"The Governor is my friend. I go with him for he is a good man."

"I know. You dang near got shot helping him one time." Tex produced tobacco and papers and began rolling a cigarette.

"I see the wild things go. First the grey one—the wolf is killed and is no more. Now money is paid to kill the big cats. Only the coyote lives because he is so wise and the deer because men want him to stay so they may hunt him. There is no place to go for me, so now I come with the Governor—though there is no more big woods with the animals."

"Cougars and bears and wolves are varmints. They kill cattle and sheep. I'd say it was good rid-dance." Tex lighted his cigarette.

"It is not good—but it is the way. Men will come—many of them—and there will be no more still nights or quiet days. Even up here they will come to live and build roads and houses and then there will be no quiet." Hopi's expressionless face bent over the dead fire.

"Well, that'll be after our time." Tex got to his feet and flexed his arms. "I'm rolling in."

Hopi Joe waited until Tex was snoring before he rolled up in his single, heavy blanket with his feet to the fire.

There was no trace of grey in the east when Tex rolled out of his blankets the next morning. The stars shone overhead and a chill wind was blowing down off the snow caps. The meadow lay white with frost in the

The Colorado winter begins for this noble buck. (Photo © Michael Mauro)

Above: *A young buck in the foothills of the Rockies. (Photo © Michael Mauro)*
Left: *Emotions run high during the rut, as two muleys battle over a doe. (Photo © Bruce Montagne)*

starlight. Tex tossed twigs on the dead fire and lighted a match. The flame of the match grew into a blaze with the spruce twigs snapping and popping. Tex tossed on larger limbs and the flames danced higher, sending sparks darting upward. Hopi Joe roused and sat up. He smiled at Tex.

"Three A.M." Tex said cheerfully.

"I'll look to the fire," Hopi Joe offered.

Tex nodded, then listened. Far up the meadow he heard the jingle of a bell as the jingle-horse swung his hobbled feet forward. "I'll round up the nags," Tex said, and made off.

Hopi Joe built up the big fire and set a smaller one for cooking. He put water and fresh coffee in the big pot and set about beating up a big kettle of batter for hotcakes. After the batter was creamy and smooth he sliced ham and set out a carton of eggs.

The ham was sizzling and a rich aroma was rising from the coffeepot as the shadowy forms of the horses came into view against the frosty white meadow. Tex smelled the coffee and the ham and began to sing lustily.

"Henna Mariar was a jaybird,
    A jaybird, a jaybird,
  Oh, Hanna Mariar was a jaybird!—"

The line ended with a whoop as Tex leaped from the back of the jingle-horse and rattled the oat pail. The horses all crowded around him while he measured out oats in nosebags and slipped the bag straps over their ears.

"Ride 'em, cowboy!" Doc had leaped from his bed and dashed to the fire, his teeth chattering and his knees knocking together.

The Governor and the Sheriff sat up and instantly followed Doc to the fire. Heavy trousers were hastily slipped over long underwear, worn for the occasion. Wool shirts followed, then socks and boots. Doc rummaged a towel out of his bed-roll and rushed off to the cold stream. Soon the others heard him blowing and sputtering.

"What's the idea of not going to bed? "Bill's head, streaked with grey and tousled like the mane of a silvertip, poked out of his bed-roll. Before anyone could answer he smelled the ham and eggs and coffee. "Might not be a bad idea, at that." He crawled out and stood on his bed until the mountain breeze struck him. "Br-r-r!" he rumbled and charged toward the fire.

"You have to wash, Bill," the Governor said firmly.

"Not me! I'm not shaving, either. I'm going to be as dirty as a coal miner when I come in." He sat down close to the fire and began shoving dishes about in an effort to locate the Bourbon bottle.

The Sheriff and the Governor vanished into the starlight toward the stream.

"Them ducks ought to get pneumonia," Bill said to Doc, who had returned and was holding his reddened hands to the fire. He poured a stiff drink and swallowed it without blinking. "Now for flapjacks and syrup."

Tex roped five of the packs upon the packhorses before he came to breakfast. He always insisted upon fixing the packs. Experience had taught him that Doc, the Governor and Dave did a poor job on a diamond hitch.

Stacks of hotcakes, thick slices of ham and two cartons of eggs vanished in record time, washed down with strong coffee. Grey dawn was just breaking when the party mounted. The Governor and Dave groaned a little as they settled into the hard embrace of the saddle, but Doc waved his hat and whooped. This was an error! The rangy sorrel was cold and jumpy. He humped his back and put his head down. For a few minutes he and Doc had it out in blood-warming fashion. Doc stayed aboard and the sorrel gave in.

As the Governor watched Doc clinging to leather and fighting the sorrel's head, a look of worry settled upon his face. Doc would be back on a diet of soda water after such a jolting, but there was no use in saying anything. One of the rules of the gang was that each man topped off his own horse on frosty mornings. Each would have been insulted if Tex had performed the usual rites of topping off the horses before allowing them to hit leather.

The cavalcade moved off at a brisk walk with Tex leading the way and Hopi Joe bringing up the rear.

Mule deer that do not face hunting pressure, such as this spikehorn in South Dakota's Badlands National Park, are not shy about wandering into areas of heavy human activity. (Photo © Layne Kennedy)

Above: *A young buck browses on desert paintbrush. (Photo © Lorri L. Franz)*
Right: *Rocky Mountain mule deer are the most common subspecies of mule deer. Ten other subspecies forage across the West. (Photo © Alan and Sandy Carey)*

Above: *Naturalist and artist John James Audubon observed his first mule deer in 1843, describing the deer he saw as a "magnificent animal." (Photo © Michael H. Francis)*
Facing page: *The muley has a distinctive, black-tipped tail. (Photo © Gerry Ellis/ENP Images)*

The horses blew noisily as they stepped off and Bill's bay nickered.

"Will this nag sing all the way up the mountain?" Bill demanded of Tex.

"They'll all quiet down as soon as we get going," Tex promised.

As they wound upward and the light grew better they saw many does and fawns, with an occasional spike buck or two-point who had not abandoned his family ways. They were high in the spruce with the yellow aspen belt well below them when Tex turned off the blazed trail and swung around the mountain and down into a sheltered meadow. Beaver lakes gleamed in the new light, terrace after terrace rising out of the little canyon. In the canyon there were aspen slopes and beaver roads, fresh and in places damp, leading down from the timber to the lakes. They entered the little canyon by way of a narrow path with a deep beaver lake on one side and a granite wall on the other.

Hopi Joe waved to Tex as the last packhorse edged between the water and the rock wall. He dropped off his pony and prepared to build a gate across the opening. The new camp was built under a great overhanging rock which formed a natural cavern ten paces deep with closed sides and an open face. Doc sat on his sorrel and beamed his approval of the spot.

"I'll bet many a caveman holed up here," he said.

"A fire out in front—family in the back—the old man with his club planted by that big rock." Dave bent forward as he spoke.

Tex was on the ground looking the place over. He had visited it many times and had taken refuge from storms under its projecting roof. He bent down and picked up several bits of stone which he handed to Doc. Doc spread them on his palm.

"Here's the evidence. Obsidian and flint chips. We might even find a stone ax or a grind-rock. We're following in the footsteps of illustrious hunters." He slid to the ground and began looking around.

The packhorses were unsaddled and the supplies tucked back under the cliff. The saddles were not removed from the other horses as the first ride would be made that morning.

Hopi Joe came up and stood looking at the cave. His face was grave, his eyes expressionless. Tex watched him as his black eyes roved over the cave.

"Coming in?" he asked.

"Yes. None of the dead are here." Hopi Joe said it slowly.

The Governor grinned at his friend. He knew the Hopi would no more sleep in a burial place than he would turn cannibal, and it made him feel better, too, to know they had not selected an ancient cemetery as a shelter.

A tarpaulin was hung across one end of the opening to keep wind and weather from the sleeping quarters. Bill seated himself on a big rock and watched the others work. Within thirty minutes the camp was ready to leave. A fire-pit had been dug and wood dragged up. Tex grinned at Bill.

"You'll build up a fire toward evening?"

Bill grunted, "Depends on how cold it gets."

Doc and Dave were fixing cold lunches to be carried in the saddle pockets. Rifles were examined, bolts and sights tested. The Governor was using a bolt-action .30-06 with larger receiver and ivory front bead to supplement his .38 Colt. Dave polished the gun grease from his lever-action, spool-magazine .270. Dave also favored the big receiver. Doc carried a scarred .250 of the same action as Dave's. The Sheriff carried a Krag upon which he had spent many winter evenings. It was cut down and restocked, the bolt was curved in and its sights had cost the Sheriff exactly ten times what he had paid the armory for the gun. Tex did not trouble to remove his .30-30 carbine from the saddle scabbard. He had used it for fifteen years and never found it wanting. The Governor grinned at him.

"Why don't you let me send you out a real gun, Tex?"

"Don't need it. Never shoot at anything over seventy-five yards away, anyway." Tex grinned.

"Remember, Tex, buck liver for supper," Dave warned.

"Yeah," Tex drawled. "Buck liver and biscuits."

Bill sat on the flat stone and watched the hunters ride away. He intended to drink moderately, rest a lot and play solitaire. Hopi Joe rode away beside the Governor. He carried only an automatic .22-caliber pistol and his bag would be blue grouse, the most highly prized of all game, for eating purposes.

The sun met them as they climbed up a rocky trail and halted to blow their horses on a wind-swept ledge. The massive, rugged grandeur of the scene around them made each man breathe softly. Rising barren and snow-choked above them, Gold Mountain gleamed in the new sun. Below lay canyons slashed out of the rocky mountainside, their blue depths always shadowy. Spruce ridges wound downward to terminate in aspen-choked hogbacks. The cross-overs were many and well marked.

"Few fellers will hunt this country—too rough," Tex said.

The Governor nodded. "Most of the shooting will be in the aspen country."

As though by command the riders spread out. Tex headed toward an open meadow above. He knew it was up to him to get the buck liver. None of the others would make a kill that day. They would ride hard and far, toughening their seats and fitting their legs to the saddle. Two-point and four-point would be ignored disdainfully. A coyote or two might be bagged, or a lion if one was flushed. Doc had a yen for bear and would certainly drive every chokecherry patch he sighted. Tex wanted a two-point or a spike with a spread. Camp meat should be tender and good eating. Hopi Joe slipped away on a grouse hunt. The Governor halted above the meadow Tex was heading toward. He watched Tex work around the meadow into the heavy timber and swing upward, his rifle across the saddle. A big, barren doe slid out of a thicket and stared down at the moving horseman. The Governor sat still watching and the doe ambled past him within twenty paces.

Tex disappeared into a hollow but the Governor did not ride on. He knew Tex did not intend going far for camp meat. Then he saw movement at the edge of the timber on the far side of the meadow. A great buck with massive spread had leaped out of a tangled mass of fallen logs and was bounding across

A buck keeps a wary eye while searching for the scent of a doe. (Photo © Erwin and Peggy Bauer)

Above: *Mule deer have been transplanted to places as far flung as Hawaii and New Zealand, though they are truly at home only among the spectacular landscapes of the West. (Photo © Henry H. Holdsworth/Wild By Nature)*
Facing page: *A Wyoming buck on his winter range. (Photo © Alan and Sandy Carey)*

a narrow neck of grass. His head was high, his sweeping antlers laid back. He looked almost red in the yellow sunlight. The Governor saw Tex sitting his horse calmly watching the big fellow make his get-away.

"Fifty yards—open shooting." The Governor smiled. "Tex would get a break like that and not take it."

Then he saw a smaller buck break cover to the left of Tex. The young buck was a two-point and he was unwary. He cut straight across the meadow heading for the ridge where the Governor sat. Tex's .30-30 came up and steadied, then cracked. The young buck broke his stride and swerved, then went down.

"Hurrah!" shouted the Governor as he galloped downward.

From far above came an answering shout from Doc. "Doe-doe-de-doe-doe!" Then Dave appeared at the upper end of the meadow and came galloping down the slope. The three met beside the fallen buck. Tex was down with his hunting knife, bleeding the kill, and making ready to dress it out.

"Doc never gets over worrying about camp meat being a doe." Dave grinned as they slipped from their saddles to help Tex.

"We'll hang her in a spruce and I'll pick her up when we come in tonight." Tex deftly slit the buck and reached in after the coveted liver. "Hog fat," he muttered.

"Doe-doe-de-doe-doe!" Doc burst out of the timber at a gallop. He leaned over the saddle horn and appraised the kill. "Horns, by guppy," he remarked.

Tex grinned up at him. "The Gov passed up the best camp meat. A barren doe almost shook hands with him."

"Tex turned down the biggest timberline buck I ever saw. I'd certainly have settled our bet if I'd been down there. Fifty yards and broadside." The Governor grinned up at the Sheriff.

"Not with that .38 of yours, boy." The Sheriff shook his head wisely.

"There's a cherry patch over on the next ridge. Let's drive it. I smell bear," Doc cut in impatiently.

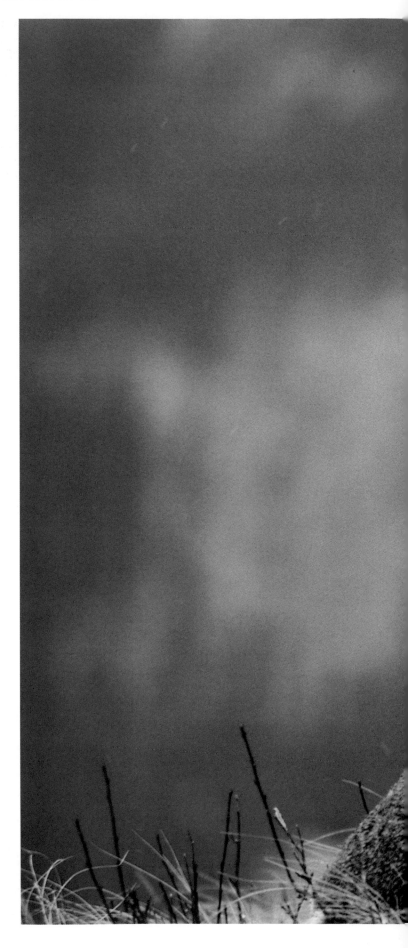

A buck rests on a wintry slope. (Photo © Michael H. Francis)

Above: *A doe in California's Lava Beds National Monument. (Photo © Henry H. Holdsworth/Wild By Nature)*
Facing page: *A healthy set of muley ears. (Photo © D. Robert Franz)*

"After we help Tex hoist his meat up into a tree." Dave caught a hind leg as he spoke.

The two-point was hoisted into a tree and the party headed across country to the cherry patch at a gallop. Spreading out, they descended upon the thicket. Tex nodded for the Governor to take a ridge which sloped out of the thicket. Doc was madly galloping around to a slide which fed into the thicket. With a whoop they charged in. Coming up with bear is mostly luck, but a chokecherry patch with frost-sweetened fruit hanging in clusters from leafless branches is a likely spot.

Doc slid his sorrel to a halt and hauled out his .250 as the others charged into the thicket. The thrashing of the horses was the only sound which came from the underbrush. Suddenly Doc's horse stiffened and leaped sidewise. A deep-chested snarl rose above the clatter of the drivers. Doc twisted his head and looked up the slide. From the top of a slab

of granite which stood above the litter of loose rocks he saw a flash of tawny yellow. For a brief moment a lean form was silhouetted against the sky as a big lion cleared the twenty-foot space between the top of the rock and the grass beside the slide, then the great cat was gone.

"Lion! Lion!" Doc bellowed.

The others made their way up to him. Their sweating, panting horses pawed uneasily as they scented the yellow killer.

"He went that way." Doc pointed up the mountain.

Tex grinned at him. "And he'll keep on going. Tonight he'll be twenty miles away."

"Too bad I wasn't on stand," Dave grinned.

"He went out of here like a teal duck coming downwind," Doc snorted.

After that the riding began in a manner the party liked. Ridges were driven, willow springs surrounded

Above: *During the winter, bucks move to lower elevations in search of food and the shelter of forests. (Photo © Sherm Spoelstra)*
Left: *Silhouetted by the setting sun, a buck rests in his forest home. (Photo © Brad Garfield)*

and combed, slides explored and wide meadows charged across. The Sheriff staged a five-mile chase down a rough slope in pursuit of a four-point which had broken cover almost under his feet. Waving his .38 he plunged across arroyos and through second-growth spruce. The buck fled in a line which indicated he intended heading for the distant San Juan Mountains, but the Sheriff stayed in the saddle and got four shots at the fleeing buck. The others did not see him again until noon. He rejoined them as they sat beside a spring eating cold lunch.

"Missed him," the Governor greeted his rival.

"Very close to the pay-off," the Sheriff said as he lay flat to drink at the spring.

"Doc is in a state of perfect bliss," Dave commented.

Indeed Doc's day was already a success. Sighting a cougar had been more than he had planned upon. Even the soda water tasted good after such an experience.

Tex left them at three that afternoon and headed down the mountain to pick up the two-point. The others drove a ridge and smoked up a big buck caught drowsing on a hillside just under a rim. The buck escaped by going downhill instead of breaking over the ridge as he should have done. Dave missed him on a downhill shot and so did the Governor. Doc smoked away at the weaving target from two hundred yards farther up the hill. After that drive they headed toward camp.

The ride in was slower. Each hunter was tired to the point of exhaustion and eager to sight the cave with its campfire. A flaming sunset spread over the sky and distant ranges were veiled in mauve and purple shadows. They saw many deer feeding at the edges of the meadows as twilight descended.

Each heaved a sigh as they rounded the rock wall beside the beaver lake and saw the gleam of the campfire. Doc was last in and closed the pole gate Hopi Joe had made from beaver-cut aspen logs. Tex already had supper cooked. Buck liver stripped with bacon was piled high on a tin platter. Dutch-oven biscuits were heaped in a kettle close to the fire where they would remain hot. The big coffeepot steamed, giving forth a rich aroma. Bill greeted them with a stiff drink of straight Bourbon and everybody except the Governor drank.

Unsaddling had been a big chore. It was done

with grim determination not to show weakness, but the saddles were not so neatly stacked and Tex made a mental note to check the hobble straps.

The buck liver disappeared and with it all of the biscuits and fried potatoes and most of the first-opened pail of jam. The dishes were washed and stacked on a flat rock. Bed-rolls were dragged close to the fire and pipes and cigarettes lighted.

"I can't forget that cat," Doc said as he drew deeply on his cigarette. He was lying, belly down, on his bed, his chin propped in his hands. He had eaten of the buck liver and bacon and was doing his best to keep it from disagreeing with him.

"Time to cut cards and see who gets the head of Wind Ridge and a shot at the white-saddle buck tomorrow." Dave yawned widely as he said it. He was thinking how swell it would be to drag his aching bones and muscles into his bed-roll and go to sleep.

The Governor had been nodding in the warm glow from the fire. He opened his eyes and announced sleepily.

"No use to cut—I'll pull the first ace."

Bill produced his deck and Dave shuffled. The Governor cut a seven of spades. Dave chuckled and shoved the deck toward Doc. Doc turned a ten of diamonds. The Sheriff reached over.

"Come on, ace," he urged softly.

His card was a five of diamonds. Dave rubbed his hands and turned the top card. It was a five of clubs.

"What'd I tell you," Doc exulted. "Have a packhorse ready to bring in the white-saddle buck, Tex." Tex grunted and went on rolling a cigarette. At that moment Hopi Joe appeared out of the night.

"Boy, you're too late for grub," Tex greeted him.

Hopi Joe grinned. "I will cook a grouse," he said and his teeth flashed white against his dark face. As he spoke he held up a string of dressed birds.

"What a breakfast! One apiece?" Dave asked.

"Yes, and one for me tonight," Hopi Joe answered.

While the others watched, he fixed a willow sapling through one of the grouse and set it to turn on forked sticks over a bed of coals. Juices bubbled and simmered as the bird slowly turned over the glowing fire. Gradually the tender meat took on a savory brown color.

"I'm about to get hungry again," Bill said as he

The Canadian sun sets on a trio of skyline bucks. (Photo © Bruce Montagne)

watched Hopi Joe test the meat with a straw.

The Indian spoke to them without taking his gaze from the fire. "I saw the white-saddle buck. You will find him at the upper end of Wind Ridge where it breaks off into Beaver."

"If he's there in the morning he's trapped." Doc sat up with sudden energy. "The ridge pitches off in a sheer cliff up at the point. There's a spruce flat full of down timber and brush close to the neck. That old buck feeds in the timber and sneaks out on the point when anyone comes. Nobody could get through that tangle without his hearing them coming."

"That is so." Hopi Joe smiled up at Doc.

"Thanks, Joe, for the tip. I'll have a mount that will show the front quarters and the white saddle."

"What time you getting up? " the Governor asked.

"Three A.M.," Doc answered as he set to work jerking off his riding boots.

"There is no need to hurry. The white-saddle buck will bed down in the fallen timber." Hopi Joe pulled a brown drumstick from the still-sizzling grouse and attacked it.

"You'll need plenty of light to get through that down timber and to shoot when you get a chance," the Sheriff pointed out.

"I'm making a rug job that will show the saddle up better." Dave was grinning as he said it.

"So you think I can't pick him off?" Doc grunted as he tugged at his left boot.

"Probably get buck fever," the Sheriff added.

After considerable cheerful chaffing of Doc, the party rolled into their blankets. Everyone dropped off to sleep at once except Tex and Hopi Joe. Tex went out to look after his horses and Hopi Joe squatted before the fire. When Tex returned he sat down beside the Indian.

"So you spotted the big boy for them?" he said in his slow drawl.

"He is old," Hopi Joe said softly. "This fall there is velvet left on his horns. Next year the white death will kill him."

"I told those birds he'd die of old age. But what's this white death?" Tex bent down to pick an ember from the fire for his cigarette.

"The snows come this winter, deeper, colder. In the beaver houses I see it and in the moss on the trees and in the nests of the little ones who live close to the ground. Winter is the great killer now as always. The big one will never battle another winter through." Hopi Joe pulled his light jacket tighter around his shoulders.

"So you're going to let Doc get him?" Tex grinned.

"I do not think so but if I do not know, then I would have a friend kill him." Hopi Joe got to his feet and smiled down at Tex, a brief flickering smile which for a moment lighted up his bronze face and lifted the impenetrable mask he usually presented to the world.

"You're a copper-skinned sentimentalist," Tex drawled.

The next morning Doc was up before Tex rolled out. He stumbled about camp, shaking and shivering. After several attempts he got the fire going and heaped wood on it. While he was dressing, Tex awoke and crawled out.

By the time the others were up, Doc was on his way to the head of Wind Ridge. Riding along under the stars with frosty meadows stretching away from the dark masses of spruce and pine, Doc let his thoughts dwell on the strategy he would employ in stalking the white-saddle buck. A stiff breeze was playing mournfully through the needles above his head and the air was keenly sharp.

Light was beginning to break into the open meadows and outline stumps and other objects as Doc reached the top of Wind Ridge. He had two long miles yet to go along the narrow top of the ridge,

Mule deer tend to be bigger in the northern parts of their range and smaller in the south, though notable exceptions exist, such as the big desert mule deer of the southwest and the tiny Sitka blacktail of Alaska. (Photo © Alan and Sandy Carey)

but the steep climbing lay behind him. As he moved along he watched the sun's first shafts strike the snowy spires of Gold Mountain. The yellow rays broke into a pink glow as they reflected from the snow. Now he saw bands of deer feeding close to the timber in the meadows. The Governor, Dave and the Sheriff, with Tex leading them, would head high up under the snow rims after the lone monarchs who never came down to the easy life of the valleys. Those big ones were strong hearted, disdainful of killers who prowled at dawn or at dusk, unafraid of the white scourge of winter, the most terrible of all enemies of wilderness dwellers.

The sun had warmed the slope, melting the frost except in patches under the spruce trees and on north banks, by the time Doc reached the edge of the little flat where the narrow hogback widened into a cramped plateau. He dismounted and hitched the sorrel to a dead log, slipping his bit from his mouth so he could feed within the compass of the reins. Loosening the .250, Doc patted it and slid open the block to make sure a cartridge was in place for firing.

He moved ahead slowly, stopping often to listen, peering ahead carefully. His memory of the spot served him well and he was able to avoid the worst of the down timber. Giant spruce towered overhead while logs lay in a confused tangle on the ground. Thick brush, weeds and grass grew underfoot around the rotting logs. Doc clambered over or crawled under the obstructions as he moved ahead. A mat of fallen leaves from the bushes made silence almost impossible.

Doc had penetrated halfway into the timber when he heard a twig snap ahead of him. Halting, he balanced the .250 and waited. Back of a leafless clump of chokecherry he saw a red-grey form move. An instant later a great buck lifted and soared over a four-foot log which lay beside the bush. His spread of antlers was amazing, but he carried it easily. Across his back and down almost to his belly extended a white band of hair. At first Doc thought he had flushed a bull elk. The .250 settled and steadied but he did not fire. He grinned eagerly. That was a pretty good snap shot, better than he had ever had before, broadside with a second's warning to get the drop, but Doc was not worried. The white-saddle buck was bounding straight toward the narrow ledge beyond

the woods, the trap where Wind Ridge pinched out on the face of a cliff.

Without worrying about noise Doc leaped after the big fellow. He was puffing and blowing as he scrambled over the last down log and raced toward the narrow ledge of rock. As he came out on the narrow point he caught sight of the big buck again. The big fellow soared into the air as though on wings and settled from sight. Doc rushed on, eager to get his open shot. He raced to the very edge of the granite lip where Wind Ridge broke off. Standing above the chasm, he looked down through the deep blue of the canyon to a meadow far below. Turning slowly, he stared about him. Gone! Vanished into thin air! Doc remembered what Hopi Joe had said about the white-saddle buck and a creepy feeling tickled his spine.

On either side the ledge broke away sharply. Sheer walls dropped away less than a foot from where Doc's feet were planted. He edged over a little and stared down, then drew back quickly. He peered over to the right with the same result. On the left he discovered a bench but it was far down.

Shaking his head, Doc walked back into the down timber. The big buck must have taken wings! He kept the .250 across the saddle as he rode back along the ridge. Tomorrow he would hunt the lesser monarchs higher up. Dave, the Governor, or the Sheriff would get a chance to solve the mystery of the white-saddle buck.

In camp that night Doc tried to tell his story in a manner which would give it a reasonable slant. The others watched him with sober faces, but with eyes twinkling. Dave had shot a fine buck high under the last broken rim close to snow line so that he was out of the contest for the white-saddle monarch.

"He just vanished, like that!" Doc snapped his fingers.

"For a moderate drinker, Doc, you see the strangest things," Bill said with a grin.

"Sure he doesn't have wings?" the Governor asked.

"Better take any snap shot you get," Doc advised dryly.

"I'll tell you just how he really acts," the Sheriff promised.

Hopi Joe, seated by the fire was smiling to him-

A raghorn buck in the Rocky Mountain Arsenal National Wildlife Refuge. Antler velvet peels away very quickly, often within two or three days in September. (Photo © Michael Mauro)

self. Tex speared another biscuit and sopped it into the grouse gravy on his plate. "Better cut the cards again," he advised. "Joe says the old boy will be right back there again tomorrow."

The cut was made at once and the Sheriff drew high card. He had a theory as to how the big boy had eluded Doc. Many times he had seen a big buck double back so close to a hunter that he could have been knocked down with a club. The Sheriff intended to keep his eyes open and his .38 ready. Dropping the white-saddle buck with his Colt would settle the question of supremacy between himself and the Governor.

The next night the Sheriff was back in camp

when the Governor, Dave and Doc returned. They greeted him with, "Where's the white-saddle buck?"

The Sheriff looked a trifle hesitant and exchanged glances with Doc before he answered.

"I got a fair snap shot. Missed. Then I figured I had him cornered so I dived right in and damned if that big boy didn't dissolve right into the air. Fact is, I saw him take off." The Sheriff waited with an air of defiance for some one to make a remark about his mental condition.

"I'd say he did just that," Doc agreed as he tossed his saddle into the grass.

"Glad you left him for me," chuckled the Governor.

"You'd better practice a bit on wing shooting," the Sheriff advised dryly.

There the matter rested. The day's hunt had been a hard-riding, tough-climbing ordeal which had not yielded a single big fellow. The Governor had missed a three-hundred-yard shot across a canyon. Doc had gotten five chances at vanishing white rumps but not a single hit.

The Governor sat down beside Hopi Joe. "Think that big fellow will be back there again after so much chasing?" he asked.

"Mebby he'll always be there," Hopi Joe suggested.

Doc turned and looked at the Indian. He said nothing, but there was a smile on his lips.

The next morning the Governor rode up to the ridge with the party. They parted at the top. Doc and the Sheriff went up the trail while Dave went with the Governor to have a look at the white-saddle buck.

Doc was riding along easily when he sighted a deer moving into a spruce stand on a knoll. Fixing the moving animal, he drew in his breath. The buck was a big fellow and he was not hurrying. Signalling to the Sheriff, Doc galloped around the hill to approach from below. He leaped from the sorrel and hitched him to a tree, then moved upward.

His calculations would have been good had the buck kept on his course. Something caused him to swing upward and when Doc spotted him he was a full three hundred yards away, crossing a little opening in the trees. He was broadside on, so Doc dropped to one knee and drew a careful sighting. The .250 roared and the buck staggered, spun half around by the impact of the bullet. Doc leaped out of the timber and raced across the meadow. The buck did not go down, though he was hard hit. He moved straight down the slope toward Beaver.

Doc knew the big fellow would escape if he got into the canyon, so he hurried on. The buck cut around the slope after descending a short distance and kept on a trail which ran parallel to the top. Doc hurried, but he could not overtake his wounded quarry. At last he slowed his pace to a walk. Left undisturbed, the buck would lie down and he could come up on him.

For an hour he tramped along. The buck was following a bench which ran along the steep slope. Doc realized that he would have to return the way he had come. There was now no chance to climb up to the top. Cliff walls rose sheer from the path. Then he saw a patch of blue ahead and knew he was coming to the end of Wind Ridge where it broke off in a granite cliff. He was sure his buck was ahead because of blood signs on the trail. Then he saw the big fellow. He was down and had rolled off the ledge, lodging against a spruce fifty feet down the steep mountain side. Doc slid ploughing down to his kill. The buck was dead when he got to him. The .250 bullet had struck back of the shoulder fairly high up.

Doc got out his hunting knife and prepared to dress his kill. Suddenly he heard a shot above him and looked up. He caught up the .250 and stood waiting as he saw a great buck appear upon the rim above. The big fellow whirled and looked back up the slope. Doc could see a wide, white saddle across his back. The great spread of his horns stood out against the sky. Then the buck gathered himself together and leaped straight out over the edge. His descent was close to, and paralleling the wall. Doc stretched his neck expecting the buck to be smashed to a mass of torn bone and hide. The big fellow landed upon a narrow shelf perhaps fifteen feet down the face of the cliff, then leaped again and ploughed to a halt in a clay bank above the trail. Instantly he crowded close against the wall and trotted up the ridge.

He passed close above Doc, but the .250 was silent. Doc was grinning to himself, and he kept on grinning as he dressed out his kill. He kept wondering, too, how the white-saddle buck had learned the daring trick. The white saddle suggested he might be part mountain sheep but that was impossible. Doc, being a man of science, knew such a thing could not happen.

The Sheriff did not trail him, so he returned to the sorrel and led him down to the kill. He struggled—and sweated—and swore, but he finally got the big fellow up on the trail by using his saddle rope. Two hours more were required to get him into the saddle, but Doc had no intention of leading any of the boys down that trail. He had plans which might be upset by such action.

The tramp in was one which almost finished